THE ANKH

African Origin of Electromagnetism

D1568863

Adrift upon an electron sea
Dying of thirst how could this be?
With water everywhere,
I search for money without a care
Never once did I stop to think
maybe it's time to take a drink

                                    Nur

THE ANKH

African Origin of Electromagnetism

NUR ANKH AMEN

AFTERWORD
HERU ANKH RA SEMAHJ SA PTAH

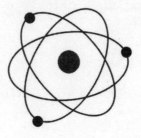

EWORLD INC.

Buffalo, New York
14208
eeworldinc@yahoo.com

The Ankh:African Origin of Electromagnetism ©1997, 1999 by Nur Ankh Amen. All rights reserved. No part of this book may be reproduced in any form or by any means including electronic, mechanical or photocopying or stored in a retrieval system without permission in writing from the publisher except by a reviewer who may quote brief passage to be included in a review.

COVER DESIGN: *EWorld Inc.*

Library of Congress Cataloging-in-Publication Data

Nur Ankh Amen
    The Ankh: African origin of electromagnetism / by Nur Ankh Amen
          p.   cm.
    Includes bibliographical references and index.
    ISBN 978-1-61759-040-5
    1. Egypt—Religion. 2. Electromagnetism. 3. Science—Egypt—
History.   I. Title.
BL2443.N87   1999
932—dc21   99-2062
                                            CI

Formally published by
A&B Publishers Group
Brooklyn, New York
ISBN 978-1-886433-12-7

Published by

EWORLD INC.

Buffalo, New York
14208
eeworldinc@yahoo.com

11 12 13 14   5 4 3 2 1
Manufactured and Printed in Canada

Relief from the Temple of Hathor at Dendera clearly shows an African Civilization in possession of light bulbs, cables and battery generators thousands of years before Volta, Edison or even Europe itself existed. It seems that no amount of evidence is sufficient to convince racist Academia to revise their established views on World History.

Acknowledgments

The Author wishes to thank the following for their contribution, although the views expressed in this publication does not represent their own.

Lee Boltin Picture Library
National Council of Churches of Christ
The Egyptian Organization of Antiquities

Contents

Introduction

DUE TO THE INCREASING INTEREST IN Egyptian science, the achievements of the Nile Valley civilization of Africa have been brought into focus. Depictions on tombs, pyramids and temples, provide a glimpse of the rich spiritual, cultural and scientific wisdom of Kemit.

These astonishing achievements point to the fact that Africa invented the Modern World. The origin of every scientific discipline, from algebra to zoology can be traced to the Nile Valley civilization in Africa. However in the face of overwhelming evidence to support an African origin of science and technology, the racist scientific community continues to deny its recognition. African Egyptologists fighting to return Egypt to Africa, have only been partially successful against the repressive colonial Academic Power that endeavors to hold our minds in slavery. The truth is the Real Estate over which we must be prepared to die, for a lie is far more dangerous, not only to ourselves but to our collective consciousness.

Now the war has taken a new turn on a different front: that of electronics. The most powerful tool of modern technology is electronics and its origin has, like most things, been attributed to the European minds of the early eighteenth century. With damaging consequences for our youth, the discovery of electronics has been claimed as the sole domain of Europeans without a single mention of any prior knowledge in Africa.

The European concept of discovery should be examined in the light of its political consequences on others, for a pattern exists which invariably results in domination and exploitation. The pattern eradicates the truth, and replaces it with lies designed to promote White supremacy. This is the prime directive: to maintain control over all other civilizations, by academic interference and distortion of traditional religious beliefs.

The discovery of the New World by Christopher Columbus is an example of this concept in action. Its awful brutality is fully documented and the results are evident on the native population even today, five centuries later. Discovery has nothing to do with original use, it is a means by which a Claim can be pursued and adjudicated by Colonial Powers.

The strategy is still used in all areas of endeavor, to allowing the expropriation of wealth, whether it be land, inventions, art or culture.

Evidence is mounting which proves that the so-called discoverers of electronics like Volta, Hertz and Benjamin Franklin, were merely Columbus's of the electronic frontier. The evidence also points to an extensive cover-up, which became imperative because of the legal aspects governing discovery. They are today known as Patent Laws. Subsequent knowledge of an invention could preclude any financial gains, rendering them useless to the new profiteer.

The cover-up and denial of prior electronic use in Africa allowed many inventions to be patented creating massive profit for the inventors and this new industry. One lie begets another and academia's role is to perpetuate these lies for future generations. However, to quote Professor Leonard Jeffries, "the truth is our most powerful weapon."

The parallel between the sudden rise in electronic inventions and European Egyptological excavations (grave-robbery) has been suspiciously ignored. It is no coincidence that the most important discovery in electronics, the pile or battery, and Napoleon's scientific expedition to Egypt occurred almost simultaneously.

Foremost in Egyptian electronics is the ☥ Ankh, and although the European Egyptologists claim that what it represents is still unknown, this is convenient ignorance.

The implication of Ankh Science is enormous and can only be fully understood through the spiritual awareness of the African, which allows him to appreciate and develop the technical sophistication with regard to its importance. I say Africans, because the ☥ Ankh is a symbol of our unique spiritual heritage. Although physical evidence of African electronic devices have long decayed or were expropriated for later examination by the plunderers of Egypt in the 18th and 19th centuries, there still remains sufficient proof of wide-spread knowledge and use in Kemit, prior to the Greek and Assyrian presence in the Nile Valley.

This book will be of special interest to those of us who have been educated in traditional electronics and science courses, and felt disenfranchised as White inventors were lauded for their contributions to a science our ancestors originated.

Author's Notes

IT IS THE AUTHOR'S HOPE IN writing this book, that serious investigation of this subject will follow, with the aim of restoring our traditional greatness and spirituality in these original African sciences.

My introduction to the ☥ ankh came in 1986 when I, as a jeweler, was asked, to make a silver ankh for a customer. I became extremely fascinated with the symbol that seem to communicate something about my ancestral past that resonated with my very soul. Trips to the local library and questions to so-called experts all gave a limited view on the subject. With the aide of my spiritual guide, Sankhamen, I investigated the Ankh for six years; studying every mention, drawing or article of jewelry. I came to the realization that the ☥ Ankh was the ultimate spiritual icon.

My traditional educational history was a disaster. I had difficulty understanding some concepts, because my professors were more concerned to label me as incompetent in science, rather than trying to educate me. The curriculum was designed to promote White supremacy and discourage deeper understanding. There was something they did not want me to know, something that seemed to arouse great fear and anxiety in them. Somehow they knew I was different, that I was not buying "the great White scientist routine;" I wanted the truth. A truth that I later found them incapable of supplying. Was I asking to be educated or spoon fed?

I decided to wean myself from the American Educational System and pursue a deeper understanding of science through spiritual discipline and divine inspiration.

Through these methods I was taken to the heights of celestial wisdom and knowledge so vast in scope, that they could not be explained in the scientific precepts or language used today. My impressions are that spiritual precepts are a higher order of the same scientific concepts but separated by a yet unrecognized form of sensory perception. It was like trying to see with one's nose or attempting to describe a scene based solely on one's sense of hearing. No wonder the spiritualists were frustrated, they could not express to anyone what they knew to be true from these intensely personal spiritual experiences.

I have come to the conclusion that we can no

longer allow ourselves to be educated in the same manner, by a system based on cranial capacity, while ignoring our superior spiritual faculties, simply because they cannot be expressed in language to the satisfaction of our academic slave-masters. Divine inspiration is a supernatural form of communication and the ultimate goal of a truly liberated African Education System, a system that I contend is still intact today. Our professors and teachers are our ancestors, alive in a realm where belief is the door and the ⚲ Ankh is the key.

What about credibility? Why do we need the Established Academic Apparatus to legitimize our theories, and why do we need degrees to expound on those we present? Why? Let the truth speak for itself.

They do not try to disprove the substance of what we are saying, instead they mount personnel attacks on us to discredit us, or worse , they will use one of our own. Maybe a respected Black Egyptologist, whose authority will be threatened by this revolutionary view of Kemit, which he, with all his scholarly acclaim could not bring to light.

The Ankh and
Popular Myth

Anyone familiar with the ♀ Ankh will tell you it is the key of life and for some that explanation is sufficient, but for others the next question is, "what is life ?"

1. *Life:*

   a: the quality that distinguishes a vital and functional being from a dead body.

   b: a principle or force that is considered to underlie the distinctive quality of animate being compare

2. *Vitalism:*

   a: an organismic state characterized by capacity for metabolism, growth, reaction to stimuli, and reproduction.

   b: the sequence of physical and mental experiences that make up the existence of an individual.

   c: one or more aspects of the process of living

3. *Biography*

   a: spiritual existence transcending physical death.

Life is harmonious coordination of energy and matter, of such sophisticated construction and efficiency as to appear divinely ordained and self sustaining.

How could an object like the ☥ Ankh come to be representative of life? The only conclusion is that the Ankh is a mechanism that possesses a living characteristic.

An examination of the word and its usage in Egypt will reveal that the Ankh meant more than organic life.

By permission. From Webster's Ninth Collegiate Dictionary 1991 by Merriam Webster Inc., publisher of the Merriam Webster dictionaries.

ankh ☥ life, to live, living

ankh- ☥ "life, stability, blessing [or, good fortune]

ankh- ☥ ever-living," living forever

ankhu ☥ human life, male.

ankh ☥ the living incarnation of God.

ankh- ☥ "to whom life is granted." life giving.

ankh ☥ 〰️• 𓏭 a living entity.

ankh ☥ •〰️𓊖 the house of life

Ankhet ☥ 〰️𓈈 the land of life, the etheric realm.

ankh ☥ 𓉐 life in a tomb.

The Encyclopedia of Hieroglyphics states:
The ankh is commonly known to mean life in the language of Ancient Egypt, where numerous examples have been found that were made from metal, clay and wood. It is usually worn as an amulet to extend the life of the living and placed on the mummy to energize the resurrected spirit. The gods and kings are often shown carrying the ankh to distinguish them from mere mortals. The ☥ ankh symbolized eternal life and bestowed immortality on anyone who possessed it.

There is no consensus among Egyptologists as to what object the ankh represents.

It is believed that life energy emanating from the ☥ ankh can be absorbed by anyone within a certain proximity. An ankh serves as an antenna or conduit for the divine power of life that permeates the universe.

The Amulet is a powerful talisman that provides the wearer with protection from the evil forces of decay and degeneration.

The Encyclopedia of Ancient Egypt defines the ankh as:

The symbolic representation of both physical and eternal life. The ☥ ankh is the original cross with a loop that was held by the gods. It is associated with Isis and Osiris in the Early Dynastic Period, and although the knowledge of what object it signified was lost, it remained a hieroglyphic symbol of life to the Christian era.

The ankh was used in various religious and cultural rituals involving royalty. In the Treasures of Tutankhamen, the ankh is explained away as:

A stylized version of a sandal strap.

Zolar's Encyclopedia of Omens, signs and superstition says:

The circle symbolizes eternal life and the cross below it represents the material plane. The ☥ ankh is called the "Crux Ansata," it is of Egyptian origin and can be traced to the Early Dynastic Period, appearing frequently in artwork of various material and in relief, depicting the gods.

It is usually held to the nose of the deceased king

by the gods to represent the breath of life given in the after-world. The ☥ ankh resembles a key and is considered the key to eternal life after death.

Its influence was felt in every dynastic period and survives as an icon possessing mystical power throughout the Coptic Christian Era.

Amen: The secret waters of the Great Pyramid.

The ankh was the key used to control the flow of water in the underground flow of the Nile, the way a tap is used in today's faucets.

The wire ankh has been used in Dowsing, which is the pseudoscience of detecting water underground.

Stonehedge: Large volts of energy have been emitted from a megalith to a wire shaped in the form of an ankh.

The ankh possessed by each god had power associated with that god. The ankh of Anubis related to the protection of the dead, that of Sekmet war, Hapi related to the living waters of the Nile and Amen, the spirit god, the breath of life. It is being suggested that the ankh box found in the tomb of Tutankhamen was actually a mirror case. Although no such mirror was found and mirror cases were not completely enclosed, as only the mirror face needed protection, it is still referred to as a mirror case.

The ankh box of Tutankhamen

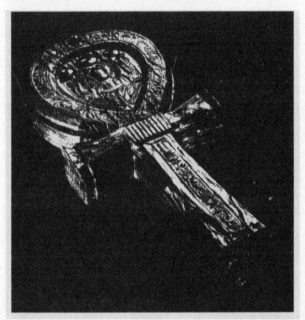

The box contained Tutankhamen's ankh device, which today is no doubt sitting in the private collection of some wealthy European collector. Some say it's in the Vatican.

One very curious theory suggest the ankh ☥ produced high pitch ultrasound inaudible to our human ear but effective in frightening wild animals like jackals and hyenas. This would have been especially useful in the wilderness at night, protecting travelers from unseen dangers.

Not only were the living protected but the dead as

well. Ultrasound has the effect of frightening insects, rodents and maggots that would devour the bodies of the deceased. By producing tiny air bubbles in the body of pests, the ultrasonic environment is very uncomfortable.

The deity associated with the dead, Anubis, is a jackal-headed god with his ears pointed up, able to hear what is inaudible to man.

Although the basic shape has remained constant, closer examination reveals subtle differences in design and construction of ankhs at different periods. The different shapes suggest refinement or varied usage.

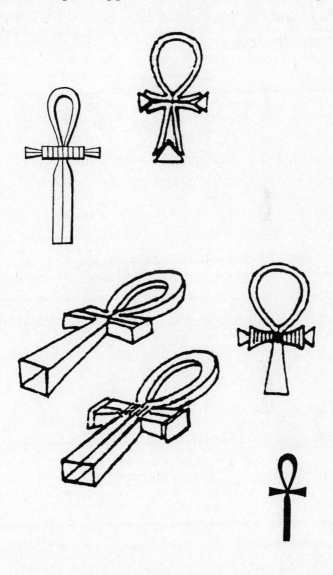

The ☥ ankh is often depicted in combination with other symbols, but it is usually attached to its power source, the djed.

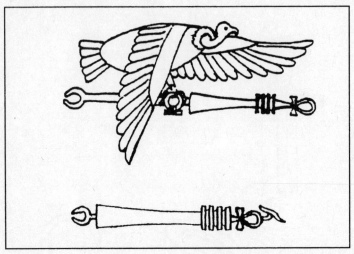

The gods Ptah and Khonsu hold this combination scepter.

Ankh Science and the History of European Electronics

THE EARLIEST RECORD OF studies in electrical and magnetic phenomena by Europeans, were done by priests of the Jesuit Schools in the 17th Century. The mysterious properties of amber, which attract small pieces of paper when charged, and the lodestone or magnet were investigated.

The core knowledge of these schools relied on the works of Greek philosophers like Pythagoras and Aristotle, who were students at the feet of the Africans in Kemit. The electron is named after the Greek word for amber.

Experimentations of the 17th Century culminated in the discovery of means by which large static electrical sparks could be produced by various contraptions which reproduced the effect of rubbing one's shoes on the carpet and touching a door knob.

An accidental discovery enabled electrical charges

to be stored in what is called a leyden jar or capacitor in 1742. This device stimulated interesting experimentation all over Europe and as far away as Japan. Electrical current could be passed from person to person in a chain and a terrific lightning bolt could be produced by the discharge.

A leyden jar or capacitor is constructed by placing an insulating material, usually wood or glass, between two sheets of metal. This invention was known 5000 years before in Ancient Egypt. Shrines were built of wood and covered with sheets of gold inside and out, then charged to protect sacred objects placed inside.

One of the most famous of these shrines was the Ark of the Covenant. Built by Moses the Egyptian, to protect the tablets of the Ten Commandments and to serve as a reminder of the presence of God. Once charged this portable shrine was potentially lethal if touched, as was evident in the Old Testament account. A priesthood specially trained to handle the shrine wore special clothing for protection and used a rod to ground or discharge the Ark. When the shrine was discharged by the priest it could be handled safely.

Exodus 25

10 "They shall make an ark of acacia wood; two cubits and a half shall be its length, a cubit and a half its height

11. And you shall overlay it with pure gold, within and without shall you overlay it, and you shall make upon it a molding of gold round about.

12 And you shall cast four ring of gold for it and put them on its four feet, two rings on the one side of it, and two rings on the other side of it.

13 You shall make poles of acacia wood, and overlay them with gold.

14 And you shall put the poles into the rings on the sides of the ark, to carry the ark by them.

15 The poles shall remain in the rings of the ark; they shall not be taken from it.

16 And you shall put into the ark the testimony which I shall give you.

17 Then you shall make a mercy seat of pure gold; two cubits and a half shall be length, and a cubit and a half its breath.

18 And you shall make two cherubim of gold; of hammered work shall you make them , on two ends of the mercy seat.

19 Make one cherub on the one end, and one cherub on the other end; of one piece with the mercy seat shall you make the cherubim on its two ends.

20 The cherubim shall spread out their wings above, overshadowing the

mercy seat with their wings, their face one to another; toward the mercy seat shall the face of the cherubim be.

21 And you shall put the mercy seat on the top of the ark; and in the ark; and in the ark you shall put the testimony that I shall give you.

22 There I will meet with you, and from above the mercy seat, from between the two cherubim that are upon the ark of the testimony, I will speak with you of all that I will give you in commandment for the people of Israel.

The Ark of the covenant

And when they come to the threshing floor of
Chidon, Uzzah put out his hand to steady the ark,
when the oxen stumbled. And the wrath of the Lord
was kindled against Uzzah; and he smote him
because he put forth his hand to the ark; and he died
there before God.

I Chronicles 13: 9

When the positive and negative terminals of a charged
capacitor or shrine where brought close to each other,
a spark could occur and if the capacitor is attached to
a stable source of current, charging and discharging
occur at a specific rate.

The high voltage necessary to charge the shrine or
ark was provided by the atmospheric potential difference between the sky and the ground. The electrical
gradient above the earth is 60 to 100 volts per meter in

fair weather and increases to 6000 to 12,000 volts per meter under a thunderstorm.

Shrines were usually placed on high mountains, natural or artificial, to take advantage of this effect. Moses was no doubt an eye witness to the ark in the King's Chamber of the Great Pyramid at Giza. The sarcophagus contained the electrified mummy of the God-King Khufu as part of a high voltage circuit.

With this tremendous power, the God-king could still communicate his will in this world from the ankhet (the other-world). So powerful was this achievement that certainty of an afterlife was firmly engraved in the psyche of Egypt, lasting thousands of years. Communication was not necessarily in words, like radio, it was a spiritual communion or revelation which was impressed upon the mind resulting in a prophetic experience.

They were communications of a highly moral nature, coming from beings who had been freed from the sinful bodily nature and viewed us as being almost like children.

The pillaging and grave robbing in Egypt continued for hundreds of years by foreigners of every description. Total disregard for the African was the only rule, so much so that the mummies or corpses were ground and boiled to make potions for sale. The European trade in mummies in the 16th and 17th century took on a feverish pace, because they were thought to have medicinal value. The melanin rich corpses of your ancestors were eaten by these savages.

By the 18th Century, the plundered skeletal remains of Egypt were under the control of intellectual scavengers in search of occult wisdom, by which they could feed the already mesmerized and addicted European aristocracy. Collectors were willing to spend fortunes to acquire these objects of antiquity, especially if they were rumored to possess some mysterious supernatural powers. Many of these curious objects are still kept secretly in private collections throughout the world.

In 1798 Napoleon recruited 167 scientists and technicians to accompany the French fleet in the conquest of Egypt. And in 1801 Volta, the so-called discoverer of the pile or battery, was given a medal and a pension by Napoleon for his contribution. The British invasion of Egypt in 1801 seemed primarily aimed at stopping the French savants from exporting anymore artifacts. It was viewed as a matter of National Security in those days.

Volta's discovery of the principles by which the

djed produced a stable electrical current, is considered to be the greatest invention of the 19th Century.

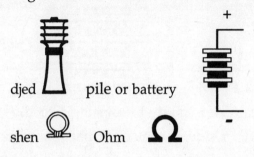

djed / pile or battery

shen / Ohm Ω

symbol for water ᗢᗢᗢᗢ electronic symbol ⟋⟍⟋⟍⟋⟍
and hieroglyph "n"
Note the similarity between these symbols.

The Encyclopedia of Ancient Egypt defines the djed as:
   The Egyptian symbol of stability. The djed is a pillar with bands across the top and base. This hieroglyphic symbol is associated with the Osirian mortuary cult practice of mummification. Serving as a powerful symbol in Egyptian magic and reincarnation, where it was used to symbolize the metamorphosis which the body underwent at death. The transformation of the physical being into its eternal celestial form.

   The djed is thought to represent the backbone of Osiris, who's sparks were as bright as the Sirius Star.

It is also associated with Jacob's Ladder.

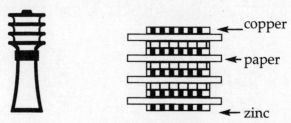

A djed or battery is made by placing two dissimilar metals on either side of a piece of papyrus soaked in salt water or acid. Greater power can be realized by increasing the number of units. For instance, a single unit of zinc and copper can produce 0.759 volts and the current has greater magnitude than that produced by electrostatic machines. Napoleon gave the Ecole Polytechnic University a battery with 600 units.

Passing voltage through all sorts of material, experimenters using these batteries were able to produce many chemical reactions and split molecules like water into hydrogen and oxygen.

Egyptologists have long suspected the use of direct current in Egypt by the many examples of electroplated jewelry and their knowledge of other chemical processes. The Egyptian word for electroplating of silver or gold is sem (sem means: a kind of, similar i.e. likeness of gold) which contains the ideographs conveying the entire process. The ⌇ uas: an indicator of electric current and ○ ⫴ nub, a gold in solution. However rather than accept the scientific evidence, these artifacts are often attributed to accidental occurrence or some still unknown process.

A good example is their promotion of iron as a Hittite technology, despite evidence of prior usage in Kemit. Chiekh Anta Diop claims iron usage originated in the Ancient Empire (2700 B.C.) and that the steel blade of Tutankhamen's dagger, could only have been produced by very deliberate means. He theorized that such a purity of iron would require the type of sophisticated processes used in modern electrolytic refinement. The ideograph for pure gold ⊓⫴⊓ is proof that the Egyptians knew that the electrolytic process led to the purest metals.

Plating was in common use during ancient times as evidenced by the many words for it. Yet no such words in Coptic (a Greek-Egyptian language) have survived, except in a reference to Alchemy from a variation of the word ⌣ ⌿ 🐍 NHB neb; to smelt or work in metal (gold).

Alchemy, the transmutation of base metals, i.e. lead, to gold, was the most sought after secret of the Medieval Period. The origin of the word chemistry, it is a reference to Egypt and the philosophy held by the Blacks concerning the transmutation of the body to an immortal spirit.

Had Egyptology been in the hands of Africans or people without a racist agenda, more knowledge would have been gathered concerning these batteries. For instance, the origin of the lead acid batteries in popular use today, may well be Ancient Egypt. Both lead and lead oxide, the elements of its construction were widely used by 3000 B.C. But what is most interesting is the word tet 𓊽 (battery or djed), it sounds like ⟹ 𓊽 teht, Copt ⲦⲞⳘⲦ the word for lead.

With the principle of the djed fully understood, the principles of the Ankh remained the greatest challenge to European scientist, however it would not yield its secrets for another 87 years.

Early attempts to unravel its secrets were made by Henry, now credited with the discovery of self- induction.

Henry reports that...

When a short wire is connected across a battery, no

spark is perceived when the connection is formed or broken. But if a wire 30 or 40 feet long is used instead of the short wire, although no spark will be seen when the connection is made, yet when broken a vivid spark is produced. The effect appears somewhat increased by coiling the wire into a helix; and it also seems to depend in some measure on the length and thickness of wire...

Henry had rediscovered self-induction, the method of producing electricity from a changing magnetic field.

Hans Christian Oersted (1777-1851) observed in 1820 the magnetic action of an electric current, opening the study of electromagnetism. He observed the deflection of a magnetic needle during a thunderstorm.

In 1842, Henry observed that the effects of sparks in one location could be detected some distance away by their magnetic effects in another location. The analogy between the rippling waves, caused by a stone dropped in the center of a pool, and the spark transmitting rippling waves in an ether-like medium, were attributed to Henry. He also noted that the effects of a single spark could be detected thousands of feet away.

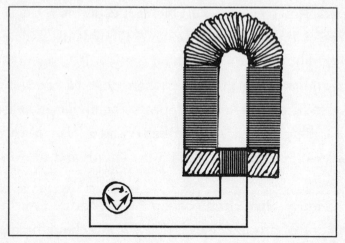

Hertz, experimenting with various sizes of loop detectors, was able to detect electromagnetic waves and determine quantitatively the effect known as resonance. Using the spark from an induction coil, electromagnetic waves could be detected in a loop some distance away. In other words, a spark in one location produces a spark between the gap of a loop detector in another location.

A hertz oscillator consists of a coil and a capacitor, made from two flat sheets of metal **B** and a spark gap **G**. One can easily see the similarity to an ankh oscillator, which produces a higher frequency because the coil is one turn or loop.

As mentioned before, the English defeated the French in Egypt, taking over the scientific explorations and

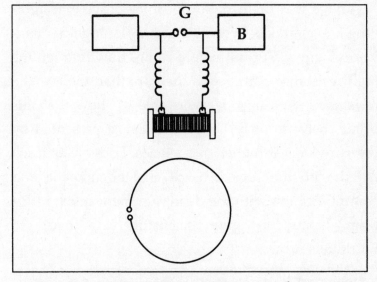

Apparatus used by Hertz to demonstrate the wave like nature of electromagnetism.

other antiquities excavated by the French. Among these were strange devices, numerous scientific and mathematical papyri and most notably, the "Rosetta Stone."

As a result of this scientific coup d'état, Newton, the famous mathematician provided the mathematical language to codify the theory of wave transmission and the action-at-a-distance properties of electromagnetic waves. Budge was able to translate the so-called Book of the Dead, and Sir Oliver Lodge discovered the properties of the ♀ Ankh.

Lodge was the first European to prove that lightning and sparks between the gap, were high-frequency discharges. Current would rather flow through the high resistance path across the gap, than the low dc-resistance wire loop. He was able to show that this occurs because of the high impedance presented by the wire loop at higher frequencies. Lodge was fascinated with the subject of psychic phenomena and communication with the dead. He spent much of his time trying to give scientific legitimacy to Spiritualism.

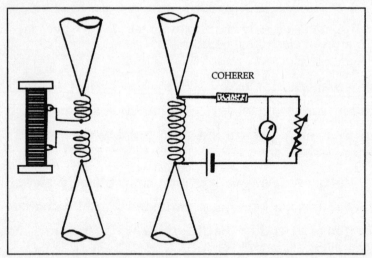

COHERER

Lodge's transmitter and receiver.

You may have noticed a set of grooves or lines in the center of some ankhs, especially the one belonging to

Tutankhamen. Well, after the discoveries of Hertz, a Professor Righi invented a very sensitive spark gap made from a sheet of glass covered with tin foil. This foil was divided into several strips by very fine razor cuts. When used in a Hertz loop detector, sparks are easily observed jumping across each gap in the foil. I would think Professor Righi was 4000 years late.

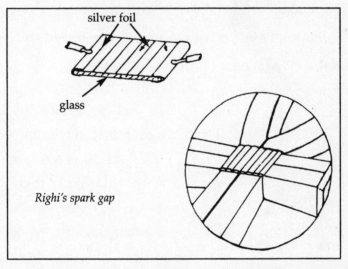

silver foil

glass

Righi's spark gap

The early telegraph and radio circuits used detectors of various construction and material. Detectors are required because the high frequency of the oscillator is inaudible. A very sensitive detector was galena (lead sulfide) crystals, some of which were found in Tutankhamen's tomb.

The hieroglyphic symbol for stone ▦ in the center of the ☥ ⊔◡◻☥, suggests the usage of crystal or even semiconductor technology. For instance, continuous wave oscillation can be produced by attaching oscillating components (capacitor and inductor) and a battery across a galena-galena contact. This black stone, kam ▭𓅓▥ a representative of Egyptian Spirituality, is the most sensitive crystal, detecting electromagnetic waves well into the infrared frequencies known as heat.

Maat with her eyes closed

If you subscribe to the belief that the ankh of a god had power associated with that god, then the ankh of Maat would be instrumental in the realm of law and righteousness. Maat is the goddess of truth, indispensable in the cause of justice. Her symbol is the feather of truth, against which the heart is weighed in the judgment. Therefore, she is representative of the solar archetype Libra.

The ankh she is holding, is the oracle of truth,

operating on a principle known as galvanic skin response (GSR) named after the Italian experimenter Luigi Galvani, who in 1750 discovered the reflex action of a frogs leg to electrical stimulus, it is widely used as a part of a modern polygraph test.

The conductivity of the skin varies with one's emotional state and what makes (GSR) so effective is how totally involuntary these skin responses are. An electrode is placed in the hand or taped to the finger of the subject and the conductivity or resistivity of the skin is measured in response to questioning. The skin is the key to the soul, portraying subtle psychological changes, it does not lie.

Vesica Piscis

Changes in conductivity of the skin alters the capacitance of the ankh, creating frequency changes as a result. By holding the ankh in this way, the emotional and spiritual responses can be communicated as a frequency modulated transmission.

A high frequency oscillator, like the ankh, has the advantage of producing high voltages at low current, so they can be handled safely. Tesla was known to have attached a high frequency coil to himself and produced corona-like discharges from his body. Luminous effects produced by high voltage high frequency coils are used today in Kirlian photography. Objects appear to have a glowing aura around them, when subjected to high voltage.

Kirlian photograph of a fingertip

The Europeans have skillfully rewritten history in such a way as to present themselves as the sole provenance of all science. Weaving a concoction so convincing, that one can only conclude that they alone have brought progress to the world. This part of their racial policy is important if they are to convince the world to tolerate their murderous onslaughts and exploitation as a necessary side effect in the cause of civilization.

One chord seems consistent in the propaganda of their discovery: a diversionary claim of ignorance and the naming of other Europeans on whose work they hold up as the basis or source material for their discovery.

Columbus used the diversion of seeking a route to

India, even though he was in possession of maps and accurate information gleaned from West African sailors who had been traveling across the Atlantic for 200 years. He claimed the Portuguese as his information source. It is the same with Volta and Galvani in the concealment of the piles Egyptian origin.

This stranglehold caused by European editorial censorship of Egyptology, is preventing the spiritual reconnection with our glorious past. Without the oppressive scrutiny of the Academic Establishment, you are free to develop your own conclusions about the ☥ ⊔◡⊏☥ using your knowledge of electromagnetism as a guide.

It is imperative for us as Africans to develop a way of teaching electronics, that is both interesting and culturally relevant, if we are ever to compete successfully in the new millennium

FREE THE PEOPLE!!

The Ankh is essential to the liberation of African peoples throughout the world. Without the Ankh and it's associated technology we will remain dependent on the inferior technology permitted by the maintainers of the status quo.

As a Free Energy Generator the Ankh represents

the symbol of our liberation. It produces electricity indefinitely without any fuel or other energy sources such as wind, solar or hydro power.

Ankhs of different sizes or capacities may be used to power boats, cars or airplanes giving them infinite range. Imagine, never running out of fuel or paying another utility bill; enjoying the freedom to live in remote regions of earth and sky as UFOs that are powered by ☥ Ankhs.

The Oscillator

A N OSCILLATOR IS A circuit which produces or responds to electromagnetic waves, usually within a range of frequencies. The circuit may consist of only a single wire, crystal or transistor semiconductor device. They respond most strongly to vibration at their resonant frequency.

Everything in nature is an oscillator and God is the spark projecting all frequencies to which everything responds. Atoms and molecules are perfect oscillators, which respond to light by absorbing and emitting at specific frequencies. Even complex organic molecules like melanin exhibit quantum states once thought to be limited to atoms and molecules. An oscillator's ability to absorb and emit energy, explains a host of phenomena which were once considered mysterious.

Oscillator: ⊙ a sine wave within a circle, is the modern symbol that corresponds to while the uraeus which is the ancient symbol, representing the serpents undulating or oscillating movements across the sand.

A circuit containing a capacitor, inductor and resistor are the components of an oscillator, which operates within a defined range of frequencies depending on their values.

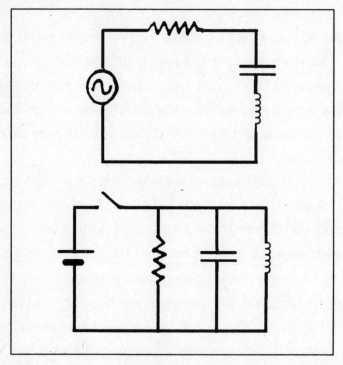

Because of the frequency-restricted nature of these oscillators they are called filters. They are also called tank circuits because of their ability to store energy.

When the switch is opened, oscillations are produced by the opposing nature of the reactive components. However, without a method of amplification in the LC circuit, the resistance eventually quells these oscillations. The result is a dampened waveform.

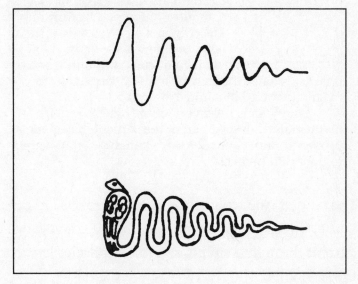

The components of a typical oscillator can be traced to the Amen Priesthood, which wielded power based on knowledge kept secret from the masses.

The symbols in many hieroglyphic reliefs are in fact elements of electronic circuit design, meant to convey knowledge of the hidden force of electromagnetism, to the future generations of this Order. These symbols would hold supreme religious significance only to the descendants of a race of Photonic Beings.

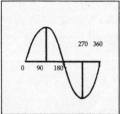

The mathematical description of a sine wave is attributed to Fourier, one of the 167 French savants who accompanied Napoleon in the conquest of Egypt. His formula describing a wave as a distinctive sum of sine waves, defined by their frequency, amplitude and phase, predates the European discovery of electro-magnetic waves by almost a century.

Like Volta's discovery of the djed, Fourier's mathematical description of the serpent, has made a profound impact on all areas of analysis from sound to quantum physics.

The scepter (rod, conductor or connector) is an important electronic component, used in the conveyance of current through a circuit and in discharging a capacitor (shrine).

The gods are often shown holding the scepter to symbolize their power over the lethal force of electrical discharge. This rod, having a loop at its base which allowed a free swinging connection, is a switch. Once planted by the loop, it was thrown against the shrine to affect an electrical discharge flow to ground.

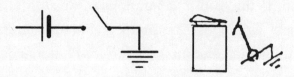

Hence the phrase "throw the switch."

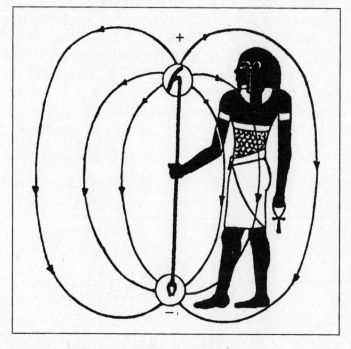

The electric field around a dipole antenna.

The mark of the beast Set (𝄐 𝄐 , a canine) and the mark of Cain are one and the same, the symbol of Christendom (+). The ion only the Setian could consider positive. While the ideograph of the earth 𝄐 is the ground 𝄐 and a source of the electron (-).

The Egyptians were fully aware of the fact that a spark produced high-frequency discharge and understood the inductive properties of rods and wires.

So Moses and Aaron went to Pharaoh and did as the Lord commanded; Aaron cast down his rod before Pharaoh and his servants, and it became a serpent. Then Pharaoh summoned the wise men and sorcerers; and they also, the magicians of Egypt, did the same by their secret arts. For every man cast down his rod, and they became serpents.

Exodus 7: 10

A conductor wrapped in coiled fashion, as a serpent is known to coil itself around a rod, is an electromagnet.

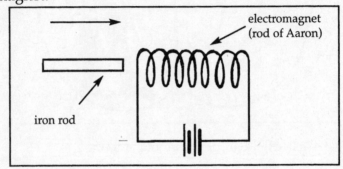

... But Aaron's rod swallowed their rods.

The Egyptian name for this coil circuit is ◿ ⌡ ≡ⁱⁱⁱ qeb, which is also the name of the multi-coiled mythological serpent ◿⌡ 🐍 Qeb. The magnetic attraction of a coil was well known to the Egyptians, 4000 years before the European named Gauss, Henry or Weber as units of magnetic force.

Another device attributed to Moses is the Helicial

antenna, made in the form of a copper serpent and suspended on a pole. It was supposedly built in the wilderness (Egypt), and as the golden calf, represented the goddess Hathor, the serpent was symbolic of the goddess Isis 𓎛 The serpent built by Moses was destroyed by Hezekiah during a period when Israel was under intense pressure from the Assyrians to abandon their spiritual, cultural and military alliances with Egypt.

> He removed the high places, and broke the pillars, and cut down the Ashe'rah. And he broke in pieces the bronze serpent that Moses had made, for until those days the people of Israel had burned incense to it; it was called Nehushtan.
>
> *2 Kings 18:4*

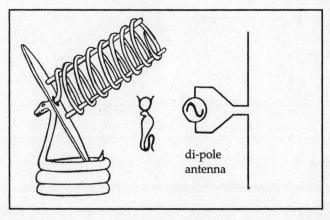

di-pole antenna

Antennas are resonant circuits which detect a specified range of frequencies. Two forms of these are the half-wave dipole and loop antenna. Used extensively by Hertz to prove the existence of electromagnetic waves, the loop antenna was used to detect the waves emitted from a dipole antenna.

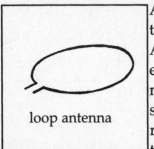

loop antenna

At the turn of the century the basic concepts of the Ankh were understood, as evidenced by the Duddell's musical Arc. The arc or spark-gap has negative resistance, where the resistance to electron flow is greatly reduced. If an oscillating circuit (inductor and capacitor) is placed across a spark-gap, oscillations are induced in that circuit.

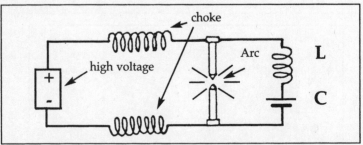

A metal loop in close proximity to the spark-gap could be excited into oscillation, due to the ultraviolet rays ionizing the air between the gap of the loop.

Perhaps the closest circuit that describes the ☥ ankh's operation is the Liebowitz Mercury Generator, invented in 1914. Using a mercury vapor tube instead of a spark-gap, continuous oscillation was produced.

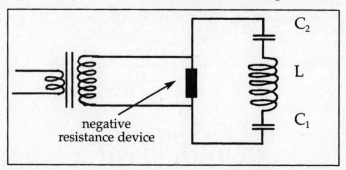

With the advent of other negative resistance devices, like the vacuum tube and the transistor, spark-gap oscillators were no longer used. They were considered noisy for the purpose of communication.

The modern equivalent of the ankh, using Tunnel Diodes.

The question still remains, whether a method of amplification existed in Ancient Kemit. An essential component in the production of continuous wave oscillation, amplification is necessary in overcoming the dampening effects of circuit resistance. It is my belief that both evacuated glass tubes (vacuum tubes) and semiconductor type active components were known and used by the Egyptians.

symbolic representation of amplification.

a representation of continuous waves

Continuous waves have been produced in circuits using an ark light bulb as an active device. And it should be remembered, that the first vacuum tubes were invented through experimentation with ordinary light bulbs.

You maybe asking yourself why the Europeans did not use the ☥ Ankh for its intended purpose, or how could an object so popular in the Nile Valleys of Africa be virtually ignored in Europe.

This is because the Europeans lacked melanin, which is an organic semiconductor, that acts as a detector (the sixth sense). Without an electric skin, an ankh is practically useless. However the principles on which the ankh operated would give birth to the many electronic gadgets in use today.

Melanin

MELANIN IS A PIGMENT IN THE skin of people of color, which is produced by melanocyte cells, and deposited in the epidermal tissue. Melanocytes are neuron-like cells which produce melanin and numerous proteins in response to electromagnetic radiation.

The production of melanin starts with the conversion of tyrosine by the enzyme tyrosinase to 5, 6-iodole quinone.

chemical stucture of
5, 6-iodole quinone

Tyrosinase is a copper-containing enzyme which catalyzes the conversion of tyrosine (an amino acid) and stabilizes the conformation of the melanin structure.

The metal ion acts as a backbone for the polymer structure of melanin, resulting in a metal-organic complex. The amino acid forms peptide-linked formations with the metal ions. The ligands are attached at the nitrogen atoms.

The proposed structure resembles a swastika, with the interactions occurring between the central Copper (Cu) ions. This complex metal compound is the only substance in the body that qualify as a organic semiconductor.

Black and brown melanin granules are oval in shape, forming a small dipole antenna. The field due to one dipole can induce a dipole in another melanin granule nearby.

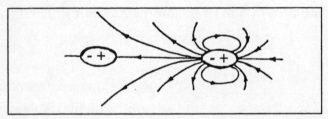

Melanin granules act as tiny primitive eyes, forming a large neural network structure, whose function is to absorb and decode electromagnetic waves. Neural-network computers are learning machines which are made with a number of receptors that can adjust their weights (quantitative properties) to produce a specific output.

The bodies of Africans contain massive amounts of melanocytes that encode all life experiences in their

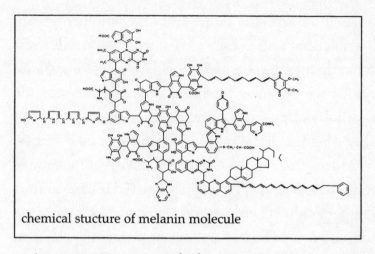
chemical stucture of melanin molecule

melanin production, with the aim of creating an actu-al- reality state after death. During life, visions appear frequently and ESP is common.

A representation of a higher form of life, in the superconducting body of Osiris (the mummy)

The reason for mummification was to preserve the skin which contained a living neural-net-work of melanin. The conductivi-ty of melanin increases with age, so Tutankhamen's mummy is more alive in the spiritual plane than our own. Consider the difference in flammability between living green trees and coal.

As a semiconductor, melanin has an energy gap. The absorption of energy is required before electrons can jump into the conduction band and make melanin conductive. An increase in conductivity increases the sensitivity of melanin to the electromagnetic world of etheric beings, astral projections and spiritual entities.

At low frequencies, the conductivity of melanin is small, but at ultra high frequencies (UHF), melanin is a superconductor. Maximum current flows only on the skin, due to the skin-effect, at melanin's UHF resonant frequency.

King Tutankamen on his throne

Melanin is the most important substance in the human body. It is an oxidized form of RNA, which enables the body to coordinate the production of Proteins needed in cellular repair. Wherever there is cell damage melanin is seen surrounding the site, functioning as a neurotransmitter in coordination with melanocyte protein production for the repair of damaged DNA.

Knowledge of the medicinal value of melanin is suppressed by the Medical Establishment in order to deny its supremacy.

The most damaging attack on African health is the promotion of albino domesticated animals for consumption. In fact only albino animals are considered domesticated. The yellow pigment in chicken and the lack of tyrosinase in albino animals, are responsible for premature aging.

Illustrates the curative properties of negative ions, the electromagnetic energy of mental concentration can be directed through the breath of life, by a competent Psychic healer.

The laying of hands on which is known to emit energy from the aura.

The Spiritual or Electromagnetic Worlds

THE MYSTERIOUS NATURE of God is central to Christian doctrine. Most believers and their preachers maintain the mystery through ignorance and confusion. The various interpretations of the Bible leaves one wanting for a simpler understanding and a more practical version of God. Despite the many scientific discoveries into the nature of the world, a separation between science and religion has prevented the understanding of anything spiritual, from an objective point of view. This separation is the result of a pathological condition among non- pigmented people, which renders them incapable of becoming in tune or sensing these higher forces directly. Imprisoned by this condition, our white ruler's viewpoint on spiritual affairs cannot be trusted despite its domination over more traditional nature-based religions of the world.

It is obvious that the early Christians' religious concepts came to Europe from Ethiopia, as evidenced by the language used to describe the spiritual realm.

ethereal   1. a: of or related to the regions beyond the earth b: celestial, heavenly c: unworldly, spiritual.

2 a: lacking material substance: immaterial, intangible.

ether   1 a: the rarefied element formally believed to fill the upper regions of space

b: the upper regions of space: heavenly

2 a: a medium that in the undulatory theory of light permeates all space and transmits transverse waves

b: the medium that transmits radio waves

ethic   the discipline dealing with what is good and bad and with moral duty and obligation.

2 a: a set of moral principles or values

b; a theory or system of moral values (the present-day materialistic)

Ethiopic 1 a: a Semitic language formally spoken in Ethiopia and still used as the liturgical language of the Christian church in Ethiopia

2 a: the Ethiopic group of Semitic languages.

utopia   1: an imaginary and indefinitely remote place 2 a: a place of ideal Perfection esp. in laws, government and social conditions.

By permission 1991 by From Webster's Ninth New Collegiate Dictionary by y Merriam Webster Inc., Publisher of the Merriam Webster dictionaries

The rise of materialism brought new language, electromagnetic replaced the word "ether," in describing the heavenly medium, thus erasing the link between spiritual and natural phenomena. The pathological condition of race caused them to enforce this separation academically and religiously, by claiming that the classical ether was unnecessary and the vacuum was somehow endowed with odd and unusual characteristics. With their strong emphasis on materialism, all electromagnetic theory was co-opted for material implementation, therefore losing all spiritual application.

Anyone displaying an interest in electromagnetic spiritualism was considered to be a pseudo-scientist and ridiculed. There were many devices which claimed to photograph, or record the voices of the dead. These ghost detectors were routinely rejected by the materialist' scientific community.

The seventies brought renewed interest in Psychic Phenomena and ESP around the world. Knowing that belief is the prerequisite to the use of ones psychic ability, the scientific community conspired to take over this research with the aim of disproving and suppressing any attempt at legitimizing this field. So most people continue to experience vivid dreams, visions, premonitions and a host of strange occurrences, which scientists refuse to recognize because of their threat to the materialistic power structure.

African culture and history are rich with examples of the unity of spirit and matter; heaven has always been our birthright. Today those faculties that put us in tune with the spiritual world are weak from lack of exercise. We have allowed the TV, radio and the telephone to replace our telepathic abilities, few now believe or would accept the notion of astral-travel.

Service to the materialist's society requires the denunciation of the spiritual. When bills are on our minds, we dream less as we focus on the depressing condition of this earthly prison, with our tormentor on our backs. The ☥ ⊔◡▢☥ is the key to the door of eternal life, strengthening our faith in a world unseen, where our souls can be free.

Osiris The First Resurrected Christ

THE CORRELATION BETWEEN the myth of Osiris and the story of the Christ have been illustrated by many prominent historians, who have shown that the evolution of Christianity is rooted in the religion of Isis, Horus and Osiris. This religion survived in its last outpost in Nubia until the Temple at Philae was destroyed by Justinian in 6th century A.D.

Although there are many versions, the essential theme of the Osirian legend, states that Osiris was once king of Egypt.

Statue of Osiris

He came to an untimely death at the hand of his brother Set, who had the parts of the dismembered body of Osiris hidden in various locations all over Egypt. Isis, wife and sister of Osiris found all the parts and was

Horus, Osiris and Isis

able to reconstruct the body with the exception of the penis, which was thrown in the Nile and eaten by fish. Her lamentations were heard by Ra, who sent his fourth son Anubis to wrap the body with bandages and perform all rites due one of his stature. Isis caused the breath of life to enter into the body by the rapid beating of her wings, whereupon Osiris was resurrected and became the king of the other world. While hovering over the body she became pregnant and later conceived a son Horus, who would avenge his fathers death.

Hence-forth all the dead of Egypt were considered Osiris, wrapped in the bandages of the familiar mummy, with the hope of resurrection in the spirit world of the ankhet ♀ 🔲 "the land of life."

If the Egyptians seemed to be preoccupied with the dead, it is from a belief that life on Earth was merely a preparation for an eternal life. The proof of this could be demonstrated by the ankh, which become the symbol of life, because of its ability to detect the energies of that realm.

Further proof that life on Earth was preparation for another life is the manner in which we dream. Dreams are our fledgling entrance into the spirit world while we are still alive. Our earliest attempt at spiritual flight are short. While dreaming the penis is usually erect (the phallus of Osiris is unnecessary) and the body is kept rigid by powerful chemical secretions from the brain; which prevent it from acting out the experience. During those brief seconds we are as if dead, yet alive in the other world.

> The days of our years are three score years an,reason of strength they be four score years, yet I labor and sorrow; for it is soon cut off, and we fly away.
>
> *Psalm 90: 10*

According to Gerald Massey's book *Ancient Egypt Light of the World* , Osiris is the Corpus Christi. The word Christ comes from the Greek word "Kristos" which means "anointed." In Egypt "krst" means; to embalm, to knot, to make the mummy.

Central in Christian theology is the resurrection of Christ from the dead. This concept has an undying appeal for the masses of humanity from the dawn of the human experience.

> The thief cometh not, but for to steal, and to kill, and to destroy: I am come that they might have life, and that they might have it more abundantly.
>
> *John 10: 10*

Acceptance of the Egyptian definition of "Krst" could put the confusion within Christianity to rest. For Christianity did not start with the Jews, but was of Egyptian origin, revolving around mummification and the spiritual resurrection of the dead. The followers of Jesus, after his supposed death and resurrection, were only later called Christians because their beliefs were similar in nature to what was practiced in Egypt for thousands of years.

Unfortunately the misinterpretation of this mystical gospel would ultimately inspire the outrageous behavior of ingesting the flesh of mummies (Krst, Christ) in hope of attaining immortality. This felonious religion let loose among a canine race, already predisposed to cannibalism, found easy acceptance in a god who offered his flesh and blood as a means of salvation.

> And he said to me, "It is done! I am the Alpha and the Omega, the beginning and the end. To them that thirst I will give water without price from the fountain of the water of life."
>
> *Revelation 21:6*

These Greek letters, alpha and Omega, have come to represent Christ.

In the original myth, Horus lost an eye in his victorious battle against Set. After his wound was healed by Thoth, he gave the eye to Osiris to eat, which vivified and strengthen him. The eyes of Horus are the sun and moon. Our sun is living water, made mostly of hydrogen that has not suffered the death of oxidation.

There is much evidence to conclude that life energy may be harnessed to prolong the life of the living. Our ancestors took full advantage of this wholistic science, allowing some to live hundreds of years. This technology predates the Early Dynastic Period in a time when the Earth, according to the Egyptian, was inhabited by demigods and kings. Obviously the Ancients had different priorities. The accumulation of wealth was superseded by a desire for wisdom and life.

The mythological story of the creation of man, recorded in Genesis, was taken from the original Egyptian story of the creator god Khnum who formed man and his Ka on a potter's wheel.

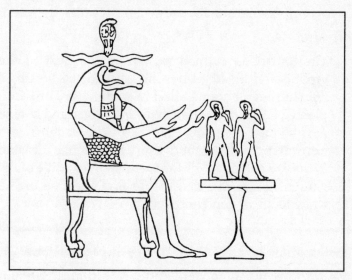

The hieroglyphic symbol which represents Khnum consists of a Tet between the raised arms of the Ka symbol and the word 𓏲𓏭𓈖 aun, which means light-tower, 🛆 another name for the God Amen.

> "Allah" is the light of the heavens and the earth. A likeness of his light is as a pillar on which is a lamp. The lamp is a glass, the glass is as it were a bright shining star-lit from a blessed olive tree, neither eastern nor western, the oil whereof giveth light, though fire touch it not - light upon light. Allah guides to his light whom he pleases."
>
> *Surah 24:35*

The Tet is the orthodox illustration of a tree and according to Gerald Massey, it represents the eternal life after death.

> The Lord God formed man from the dust of the ground and breathed into his nostrils the breath of life, and man became a living being. The Lord God planted a garden in Eden away to the east and in it he put the man he made. The Lord God made trees to grow up from the ground, every kind of tree pleasing to the eye and good for food; and in the middle of the garden he set the tree of life and the tree of the Knowledge of good and evil.
>
> *Genesis 2:7-9*

Notice that the tree of life was not planted but set in the middle of the garden. After Adam and Eve ate of the fruit of knowledge of good and evil they became knowledgeable.

> The man has become like one of us, knowing good and evil; what if he now stretch forth his hand and takes the fruit of the tree of life also and eats it and live forever? So the Lord God banished him from the garden to till the ground from which he has been taken.

> *Genesis 3:22*

The tree of life was no ordinary tree.

> She replied. "We may eat the fruit of any tree in the garden. But the tree in the middle of the garden, we may not eat or even touch it lest we die."

> *Genesis 3:2*

The Tet is a high voltage power source, touching it may have been lethal to those without knowledge. Adam, who now possessed knowledge knew that the ankh portion of the tree was a high-frequency source that could be handled safely.

Tet ⊜ ◊, ◿ ◊ ◿ ⊔ fruit tree., Danger do not touch.

Now we have come full circle and in our midst is the tree of good and evil, the modern computer and the Tree of Life, which is the Ankh Science of our Spiritual Nature. The moral question faces our generation, whether to trust Satan's path or the path which leads to Eternal Life as gods.

For it is not simply a question of a machine, but the programming of falsified information aimed at seducing you from your Divine Nature.

Who said you were ignorant, for you were created clad in Divine Wisdom and light.

The depiction above shows Ra, Sun-god and his etheric double, Amen-Ra, the hidden force behind the sun. Our sun has a surface temperature of 6000 degrees, yet its corona (spirit or aura) exceeds 2 million degrees. The difference in temperature is caused by laser-like effects produced by the strong electric and magnetic fields within ionized gases over the highly reflective surface of the sun.

King Tut is also depicted with his etheric double and like Ra his name Tutankhamen expresses the hidden source of life. All living systems have electromagnetic phantoms. The phantoms of atoms and molecules are called photons, they are the essence of nuclear life, governing the energy states of the material world.

The ankh is held to the nose area because of its sensitivity to electromagnetic waves. The area between the fifth and sixth chakra is centered around the nasal cavities, where a massive quantity of neural receptors, responsible for the sense of smell, are exposed to the environment. The sensations are often confused with sound because of their proximity to the ears, sounding like the noise you hear from a TV set tuned to an unused channel or like the sound of the ocean.

Sensitivity can be increased and with practice one can detect the presence of high frequency waves close by. Some highly spiritual people, are so sensitive to these waves, that their neurons can demodulate radio broadcasts, causing them to hear voices. Many end up in psychiatric wards because they hear voices other can't.

The gods, who are a spiritual race of photonic beings, made man in their own image and likeness, to serve them on Earth. However man became aware of his own divinity and sought to be like the gods while in the flesh.

The story in Genesis also relates the longevity of Adam and his sons, whose average life span was 900 years.

> Then the Lord said, "My spirit shall not abide in man for ever, for he is flesh, but his days shall be a hundred and twenty years"
>
> *Genesis 6:3*

So it is the spirit (photonic or electromagnetic energy) which gives man the ability to live an extended life span. A tree deprived of a important nutrient like sunlight or water would wither and die in a shorter time. Without this vital ingredient we grow old and die prematurely.

The first signs of aging are apparent in the skin and is related to some melanin dysfunction. There is an increase in yellow pigment and among Caucasians there is premature wrinkling and melanoma. If the resonant frequency of melanin was known, the appropriate energy could be absorbed to vitalize the skin and delay aging.

Electromagnetic radiation may cause cancer among Whites because non-pigmented skin, has no defense against a high frequency wave which penetrates deeply in human tissue.

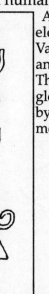

A drawing of the World's First electronic clock, built by Nile Valley Africans to represent their ancestral spirit Tet Ankh Ka Ra, The Ankhi (Khnum, chronos). The glowing globe was slowly rotated by the precise electromechanical movement of the arms.

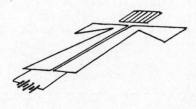

The Tree of Life provided sufficient power for the creation of electromagnetic radiation (angelic or spiritual beings) and the rotation of the world. The Egyptians not only knew the world was round, they knew the force which turned it was a perpendicular electric and magnetic field. They used elements of electronic circuitry to represent the spiritual nature of life. The circuit on the right of the tree is a relaxation oscillator, charging and discharging through the spark gap, to provide excitation for the loop circuit in the figure below. A minimum of 300 volts is required to produce a spark across the gap.

The relaxation oscillator is an inefficient method of excitation, because the discharged cannot be synchronized. However, with the use of kam (galena), a more effective continuous wave excitation oscillator can be made that requires significantly lower voltage.

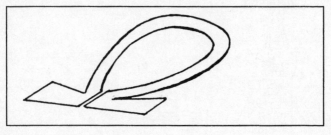

The loop and plates above are also a tank circuit which is shunted across the gap and capacitively coupled to the input resonant circuit. This transmitter radiates UHF power to ankhs of comparable size within the vicinity.

The spark was considered to be an indication of Gods presence because within a spark all frequencies are generated, therefore, all circuits are compelled to respond. The large capacitance of the shrine or ark could provide powerful sparks of lightning sufficient to excite an ankh into oscillation, especially when this discharge was through the gap of a transmitting ankh circuit.

A circuit consisting of a loop and plates could also provide lighting at night or in the darkness of the tomb. It has always been a mystery as to what method of lighting was used to allow those intricate paintings to be produced on the walls of some of those tombs. No soot was found on the ceiling suggesting that some other method besides the torch was used. Again we are asked to believe it was done with mirrors reflecting sunlight, because the truth of electric lighting in tombs would suggest widespread use similar to our modern use, but superior, because power would be wireless transmitted..

The pectoral of King Senusret II embodies the spiritual and scientific principles governing the universe. The ankhs illustrated have coils on either side of the loop, and Heru (falcon) is standing on the senk Ω , a divine light.

When this type of ankh was constructed and attached to a battery, it operated like a motor and produced high voltage spikes at audible frequencies.

The coils on both sides of the loop, form an electromagnetic switch, which switches on and off under the influence of magnetic attraction and the flexibility of the loop. The high voltage produced is a result of the sudden interruption of current flow through the coil.

This by itself did not seem strange, for on closer examination of the output, it was discovered that the

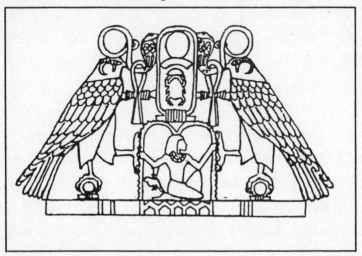

output power exceeded the input power. With the use of rectifiers and rechargeable batteries, the excess power kept the ankh in a state of perpetual motion. The latent energy within the magnetic field was harnessed to produce electricity.

The kneeling figure in the center of the pectoral is Heh the god of Eternity, holding the notched chain of infinity.

This type of ankh was undoubtedly the power transmitter for the loop circuit of the senk.

snk , to see the light

snk light rays

snk , night or darkness (note the senkh is upside down over the symbol for sky)

sen Ω or Ω kh senk or senkh.

sen means, similar, dual, two or alike.

Similar to today's fluorescent lamp, the senk was used extensively before the numerous invasions put this light of Egypt out forever.

Since there are no known surviving examples of the senk, its basic operation can only be extrapolated from fluorescent light theory and examples depicted in Egyptian Art. The primary elements of the senk's construction are:

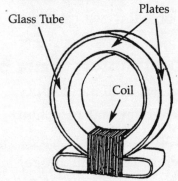

Glass Tube
Plates
Coil

1. partially evacuated glass tube

2. coil or loop (inductance)

3. plates (capacitor)

4. DC. voltage

A partially evacuated glass tube can be made to glow when placed within a rapidly changing electrostatic field. The air in the tube is ionized by the presence of high-frequency oscillation in the coil and plates, at 10 to 50 MHz. The ionized gas in the tube becomes conducting and establishes direct current flow from the battery through the tube, further increasing the intensity and duration of the glow.

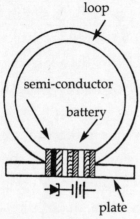

loop

semi-conductor

battery

plate

The ionized gas tube of the senk can be adapted for use as a diode (rectifier) or as an active device by exploiting it's negative resistance for amplification. By adding an extra set of plates to isolate the DC voltage, the senk could easily be modified to produce continuous wave oscillation. However since the Egyptians had knowledge of galena, it is likely that the vacuum tube was abandoned in favor of more efficient semiconductor technology. If all the components of modern radio transmission and reception were known and used in Kemit, 4000 years before their re-emergence in this century, then the super technology of the UFO's need not have come from other planets, but could have developed right here on Earth.

These are the questions which will arise to disturb the status quo if knowledge of ⚥ ⊔⌀⊏⭞ science is made public. It would necessitate a complete re-examination of Kemitic religion to explain the connection between the African and these electromagnetic circuits, which were of such high spiritual significance. This would provide a direction for research into what we truly are as a people.

The atmosphere is a rarefied ocean inhabited by numerous spiritual entities living in realms which vary in activity levels between night and day or during cloudy weather conditions which causes the spirits to take on a higher density.

The electronic circuitry of the Egyptians was used to facilitate greater contact with the spirit world, known as the Kingdom of Heaven. The lords of this Kingdom are called the "grays" and many consider them negative aliens because of the fear they arouse and their enigmatic behavior.

"The fear of the Lord is the beginning of wisdom."

Ankh Circuits

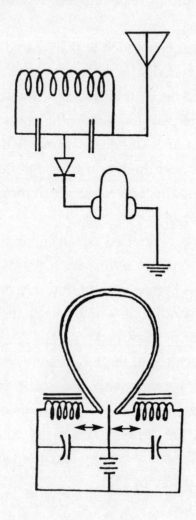

Ankh Circuits continued

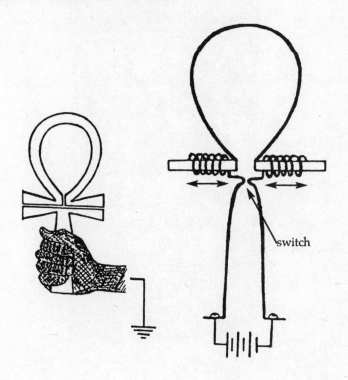

switch

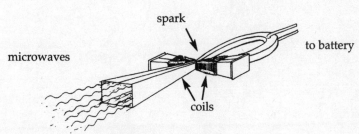

spark

microwaves

to battery

coils

The War ankh of Sekhet

83

THE ANKH ☥

84

The Heavens

A LTHOUGH THE EGYPTIANS considered heaven to be
the abode of the eternally blessed, it contained
all the elements of a blissful earthly life. The dead
were usually buried with their earthly possessions
and provisions to sustain a life similar to their earthly
one.

Everyone seems to agree that this realm is located
in the sky above the clouds somewhere, but no one
wants to specify its exact location. Here also, the separation of matter and spirit create

the usual confusion characteristic of modern religious theology and the materialist scientific aristocracy. If both spiritual and scientific evidence concerning
heaven are examined objectively by someone with a
unified perception, they would conclude that heaven
was in the ionosphere. Our ancestors, who were not
afflicted with this modem schism, knew this also.

In the beginning God created the Heavens and the
Earth.

Genesis 1: 1

The aureole of the Earth created by the breath of Ra.

The Egyptian symbol of this Creator-God Khnum is the most profoundly esoteric, containing all the elements which could explain the nature of divine existence.

This is the god that created night and day by the rotation of the earth and made man on this revolving potter's wheel.

⬭ -island vacuum glass tube ... au

∿∿∿ -breakdown discharge, "N" water, aurora.

⊔ -Ka, spirit, power, image-double.

⬭∿∿∿ -Horizon, the God Amen, aun; which means lamp or light post

▯ -Tet, djed, battery or voltage Osiris, Jacob's ladder.

As we have discussed before, the evacuated tube provides an easy path in the flow of electrons, creating the ionization and negative resistance used for continuous waves, and glowing when these electrons and ions recombine to form neutral atoms.

All these activities occur in the near-vacuum of the ionosphere, which is a region of high electron density, about 300 km above the Earth's surface. This layer is maintained by ultra violet radiation and high energy particle emissions from the sun. The high voltage (potential difference or electric field) between the earth and the ionosphere, represented by the Tet, is responsible for the rotation of the planet. This is due to the Earth's magnetic field being perpendicular to that electric field and in exactly the same way as the force which rotates the shaft of an electric motor created. The four bands at the top of the Tet represents the fact that the ionosphere is divided into four layers, the two uppermost levels F1 and F2 merge into one layer at the first hour of the Tuat (night).

Because of its high electron content, this layer reflects electromagnetic waves, allowing extended range to radio transmission.

And he who talked to me had a measuring rod of gold to measure the city and its gates and walls. The city lies foursquare, its length the same as its breadth; and height are equal. He also measured its wall, a hundred and forty-four cubits by a man's measure, that is, an angel's

Revelation 21:15

Khnum at his potter's wheel fashions a person out of clay. One figure represents the physical body while the other represents the spirit. Both came together to create one new being.

The description of the measurement are those of a sphere whose height is defined by the cut-off frequency of 1,440 Mhz. Because the measure of a man, that is of the angel is the Ka ☥, ten million.

And he dreamed that there was a ladder set up on the earth, and the top of it reached to heaven; and behold, the angels of God were ascending and descending on it! And behold, the Lord stood above it and said, "I am the Lord, God of Abraham your father and the God of Isaac; the land on which you lie I will give to you and to your descendants; and your descendants shall be like the dust of earth ...

Genesis 28:12-14

Heaven   Earth

Genesis Chap. 1-1
And the spirit of God was moving over the face of the waters.

The word "ankh" also means mirror, "that which sees the face," in the language of ancient Egypt.

Chap. 2-7
then the Lord God formed man of dust from the ground, and breathed into his nostrils the breath of life; and man became a living being.

Genesis Chap. 1-27
So God created man in his own image, in the image of God he created him; male and female he created them.

An

Phonetic Value	Hieroglyphic character	Meaning of the ideograph
ankh	⚲	life
n	〰〰	water
kh	⊛	dust (symbolized by a sieve)

examination of the word ⚲〰⊛ankh, reveals the nature of our earthly and heavenly incarnation in the eternal cycle of life. The word contains three ideographs, each representing an aspect of the Trinity, Father, Son and Holy Spirit. If you can accept the concepts ... Our

Father who art in Heaven,... I and the Father are one and... Son of man, you will be well on your way to an understanding of eternal life.

From the Egyptian point of view,⁰ ⌒ ;(pet) heaven was made from a material called 𓂋𓏏 𓊵𓏥 baa. This baa (baa; metallic substance i.e. black meteoric iron) was known to have metallic properties such as conductivity and reflectivity.

The ionosphere is a mirror image of the electromagnetic emissions from the Earth, no matter how faint. The spiritual characteristics of every object on Earth is duplicated in Heaven, because their emissions cause the electrons there to vibrate in such a way as to emit an exact electrical image of all earth transmission.

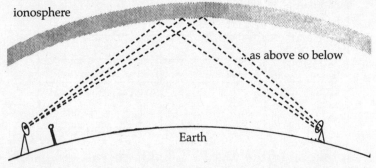

ionosphere

:.as above so below

Earth

The body was preserved with the knowledge that its electromagnetic nature would continue to be reflected in the Heavens. The concept of a spiritual abode in heaven is as perplexing to the materialist of today as it was in the time of the Messiah. In John chapter 3, the Messiah attempts to explain to a White man why he cannot go to or understand heaven.

> Jesus answered, "Truly, truly, I say to you, unless one is born of water and spirit, he cannot enter the kingdom of God. That which is born of the flesh is flesh, and that which is born of spirit is spirit. Do not marvel that I said to you, 'You must be born anew.' The wind blows where it wills, and you hear the sound of it, but you do not know whence it comes or whither it goes; so it is with everyone who is born of Spirit." Nicode' mus said to him, "How can this be?" Jesus answered him, "Are you a teacher of Israel, and yet you do not understand this? Truly, truly, I say to you, we speak of what we know, and bear witness to what we have seen; but you do not receive our testimony. If I have told you earthly things and You do not believe, how can you believe if I tell you heavenly things? No one has ascended into heaven but he who descended from heaven, the Son of man. And as Moses lifted up the serpent in the wilderness, so must the Son of man be lifted up, that whoever believes in him may have eternal life.
>
> *John 3:5-14*

It would be fruitless at this point to attempt to untangle the enormously confusing theology of the Trinity proposed by Whites who, having discovered themselves excluded, sought to deny the Divinely Blessed the knowledge of their birthright. The secret ingredient, for which our race has been made to suffer is melanin, the dust of the Kha. The word Kha ranges in meaning, from dead body or corpse to powdered medicine or simply the dust of the dead.

Allow me to digress for a moment to examine the use of dust in the early days of radio. A phenomenon, which permitted the detection of radio waves, was the response of dust particles to electromagnetic waves caused by a spark. Particles of dust tend to stick together (coherence) aligning themselves in such a way as to increase the current flow in a certain direction. The early rectifiers, known as coherers, were made by filling a tube with an electrically responsive dust or filings, (See Lodge's transmitter and receiver). When there was a passage of electromagnetic waves the coherer would conduct, however once aligned they were no longer responsive and needed to be tapped periodically to loosen the particles to respond to the next incoming wave. This is the reason why the dreamer's body must be kept rigid, like the dead, for movement disrupts the alignment reducing conductivity.

Christ said to Mary, "Touch me not, for I am not yet ascended unto my father."

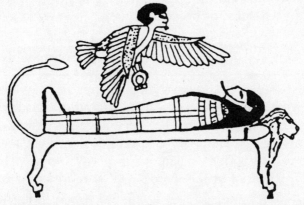

The senkh held by the Ba represents the electromagnetic emissions of the Kha.

The majority carriers (type of charge transport) of melanin are electrons as opposed to (+) holes. Therefore, in the Judgment of Osiris, described by the Millikan's oil drop experiment, the etheric body rises.

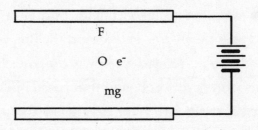

In Millikan's oil drop experiment, an electrically charged oil drop is suspended between two plates by the upward force of an electric field against it's weight mg.

Who Knoweth the spirit of man that goeth upward, and the spirit of beast that goeth downward to the earth?

Ecclesiaste s 3:21

The confusion as to the direction of charge flow displays Greek ignorance and Egyptian wisdom. Electrons flow from the so-called negative potential, known as the cathode, which canes from the Greek word "Kathodos" meaning 'the way down'. The Egyptian root of the word "Ka," is represented by the raised arms ⊔ representing the true direction of electron flow, from the ground upwards.

Each melanin granule is a tiny feather and, when energized by the ankh of levitation, the gods were given the power of flight.

The ankh of levitation was related to the goddess of the Upper Kingdom, the Divine Vulture. These vultures are often seen soaring around large clouds during a thunderstorm. The reason for this behavior was thought to be related to upward convection currents of air. And it was believed that these birds used these currents to attain great heights without effort. This assumption neglected the fact that thunderclouds possessed strong electrostatic charges which exerted a force of attraction on the birds in the same way that a charged plastic comb attracts small pieces of paper.

The goddess Nekhbet represented this principle, by which the Messiah was taken up into the clouds. By holding a high frequency emitter like the tet-ankh scepter, one could soar into the sky as the Medieval witches were said to do. At sufficiently high frequencies, the dipole of the melanin granule cannot respond rapidly enough to remain in step with the changing electric field. Therefore, a displacement current arises and the granule behaves as a dielectric, subject to the force of electrostatic attraction and repulsion

The winged serpent is the most compelling argument in the link between spiritual and electromagnetic phenomenon. While representing all the elements of airborne electromagnetic wave transmission, it evokes the wisdom and spirituality associated with Isis.

SETI (Search for ExtraTerrestrial Intelligence)

In October 1992, NASA will engage in the study of the heavens under the guise of a search for extraterrestrial intelligence in the galaxy. This project, with the very Egyptian sounding acronym, will use the World's largest radio telescopes and advanced multichannel scanners to canvas the sky in an attempt to discover the source of angelic communications.

It is no coincidence that the frequencies of interest to these researchers is around the 21 cm wavelength of the constituents of water (hydrogen: H and hydroxyl: OH), called the "water hole." This is the most prudent choice since the Messiah referred to these beings as composed of water and spirit.

These beings have the some color as the clouds, a glowing gray, and it is said that their appearance is like unto the "the sons of men," that being like children.

Despite the sophistication of the computerized equipment, the project is doomed to failure. Even if angelic communications were detected among the noise of terrestrial transmission, the language of the angels is unknown. I am not suggesting that communication with Angelic Beings is impossible. What is required is nothing less than Ankh Science in the hand of the Oracle.

The synthesis of amino acids (the building blocks of life) under the condition of a primordial atmosphere, with the use of electrical discharge, confirmed the existence of extraterrestrial life. If the chemical composition of amino acids (hydrogen, oxygen, carbon, nitrogen and other trace elements), can be found

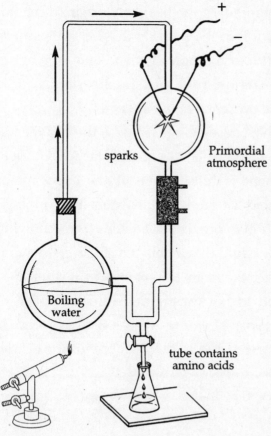

in the upper- atmosphere, then why should life be limited to the earth. The synthesis of more complex molecules (protein and nucleic acids) by linking together amino acids, involves the bonding of an amino group (H_2N) and an acid group $(COOH)$. The C—N bonding results in the removal of (H and OH) a water molecule, exactly what SETI is searching for. In this hospitable environment, of the heavenly ocean, the holographic projection of the recently dead is reconstructed, giving birth to the Son of man. This is what is meant by the return of Christ in the clouds, now revealed in the present age of Aquarius.

It is said that these beings traverse the heavens in boats or barges. These UFO's are the Fishers of men. The Government is fully aware of the existence of these beings, and has launched an extensive campaign of disinformation to prevent its citizens from knowing the truth. How could they explain to their people that the lowly Africans are merely beings in a caterpillar stage, destined to be transfigured into an image of splendor and glory. Creatures whose total existence is so eloquently expressed in the life cycle of the Scarab beetle.

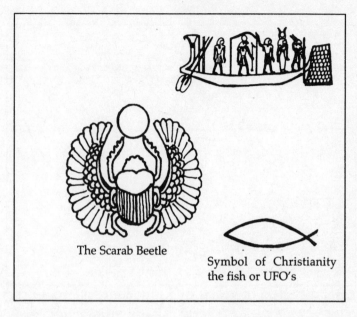

The Scarab Beetle

Symbol of Christianity
the fish or UFO's

The Scarab, symbolic of the god Kheper 🪲◇⟨🗿 is a dung beetle commonly found in Egypt. It. is usually seen rolling a ball of dung which contains it's larvae, around the countryside, creating in the mind the Egyptians an analogy with solar orbit. In Egyptian cosmology, the universe is represented as a cow called Nut.

The ball of cow dung is obviously the earth, although the European Egyptologist would like us to believe that our ancestors were as ignorant as theirs were of the Earth's orbit of the Sun.

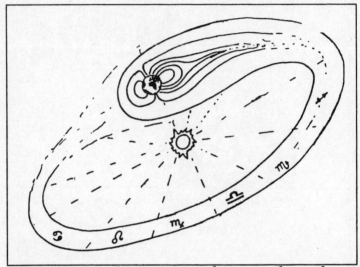

After a period of gestation in the ionosphere, the spiritual body returns to it's astral homeland, one of twelve regions, from which it came. There it will find a glorious existence beyond description, an existence where there is no night only day and it's every desire will be fulfilled in Amentet.

African Astrophysics

THE THEOSOPHICAL CONFLICT between the Big-Bang and the Steady-state model of the universe, is unresolved after 4000 years. It is deeply rooted in the Osirian and Amenite perspectives concerning the origin of the universe.

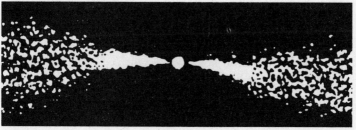

Fig. 1 Radiograph of a typical radio galaxy with jets projecting from its whirling black hole nucleus.

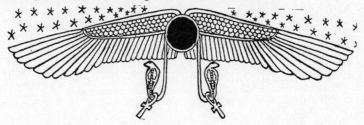

Fig 2 The twin serpents illustrate the unique feature of a radio galaxy which appear as two separate radio sources.

Osiris, God of continuity through the resurrection of the dead, is the Steady-state universe. A philosophy which arose from the African's view of himself as a reflection of the God Osiris, the Ultimate Black. The Ancient African Astrophysicist, studying the universe, also looked inside himself and found that the connection between melanin and the black hole, was the electron (the breath of life 4).

The Grand Unification Theory, which eluded Albert Einstein, has already been solved. The Africans discovered that subatomic particles, like the electron, were created when ordinary matter (energy) passes through a black hole. However, since the Europeans cannot accept Osiris, their scientists have sought diverse theories in order to circumvent the truth of an all powerful Black God.

African Plasma Physics

In the original myth, Horus lost an eye in his victorious battle against Set (Typhon, typhoon). After his wound was healed by Thoth, he gave the eye to Osiris to eat, which vivified and strengthened Him.

This myth, handed down from Ancient Times, relate the events occurring in the eye of a radio galaxy. Where stars and planets are swallowed by the central black hole and resurrected as fourth-dimensional matter (plasma).

A plasma is characterized by its high electron content. About 95% of the matter in the universe is in this state. A low pressure gas plasma need not be strongly ionized to respond to or produce electromagnetic effects. Black skin, which is composed of a layer of organic semiconductors can be considered a plasma or fourth dimensional matter. And since neuro-melanin and melanocytes are the basis of higher mental activity, it stands to reason that our moral nature is an expression of a more direct contact with God through the spirit. In other words, melanin is your link with the Universal Mind of God and morality is the

Osiris

Universal Law of reconciliation characteristic of our God Osiris. Osiris is the God of Judgment and the cross-road, whether to go right or left on the Path that leads to Him and Peace in the eye of the storm. The Egyptian symbol of a plasm ∿∿∿ is the same as "n" or water, but it must be considered as living water. It is also illustrated in the symbol of the aurora (∿∿∿) which most people can recognize as an electrical discharge in what is now called a cathode-ray tube.

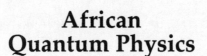

African Quantum Physics

SINCE THE DISCOVERY of the electron, modern physicists have found themselves in lockstep with a more ancient reality already defined by our African ancestors. The Tuat is the fourth- dimensional world of the electron and the core of the particle- wave paradox in quantum physics. Only the names have been changed to protect the guilty.

Our present reality is defined by the speed of light, beyond which nothing material can be transmitted, however in the actual reality world of the Tuat, the eye of the Ka sees another light. The light described in the Quran as 'light upon light' and in the Bible as an incomprehensible light that shines in darkness. The Bible is replete with descriptions of this immaterial world, providing a source for physicists, who behind closed doors, are probing the tenents of spirituality in search of answers.

> But, beloved, be not ignorant of this one thing, that one day is with the Lord as a thousand years, and a thousand years as one day.
>
> *2 Peter 3:8*

Here the existence of a non-local reality is defined by a difference in time reference. For if a thousand years is as a day, then something is traveling 365,000 times faster.

The intermediary between this world and the Tuat is the electron, the substance of the soul. It is indivisible, eternal and connected to the mind of God. This alternate reality can be understood in the analogy of the whale, whose dorsal fin emerges when the whale surfaces for air. What we observe is the point-like character of the electron or fin, but beneath the surface lies the greater glory of the whale. The Ka, which surfaces periodically from the sea of eternity, is represented not only as a particle but also a wave (the mythological serpent ◁ ⅃ ⓖ Qeb. The human body is merely the skin of this mystical serpent which is shed periodically and in which the god walks upon the Earth.

Nur Ankh Amen
The Religious Institute of Kemitronics.

The Science of Kemit

T HE RELIGIOUS CONCEPTS of Ancient Egypt were structured on scientifically verified electromagnetic theory, not unsubstantiated traditional beliefs, as ours are today. Separation of science and religion is a modern phenomenon where clashes between cultures in a shrinking world, force compromises with the perception of truth.

Most of us are unprepared to cope with the idea of a superior African science. Years of slavery and colonial domination have damaged our belief in the ability of our race to have accomplished these feats of mental genius. In spite of the pyramids and other colossal monuments, which are a testimony to our greatness, most of us are still in disbelief.

Electromagnetic religion in Kemit can be seen to have played a role in the evolution of monotheism during the reign of Amenhotep IV in the 18th Dynastic Period. The reason for the conflict between the polytheistic doctrine of the past and the singular universal god Aten may have been the result of the discovery of a new source of electromagnetic radiation called Cosmic Background Radiation,

In 1964, experimenters at Princeton University studying the possibility of leftover radiation from the "Big-Bang," discovered the universal microwave radiation hypothesized by Akenaten 3500 years before. The Aten was represented by a disc with many rays ending in hands holding the ankh (symbol of life). Because this source of radiation was universal, it was difficult to depict, therefore, the instrument used to detect its microwave emissions was used.

The Disk of aten ☥ was an ancient solar device, used to focus sunlight to a point or beam of extreme intensity. These large domed disks were made of highly polished metal (the word aten means mirror) to concentrate the heat of the sun on a focal point for a variety of uses, which include the splitting of large stone blocks. A stone block was exposed to a narrow beam and, when heated, cold water was poured causing the stone to split in precise dimensions lines.

With the rise of the Amenites, the technology concentrate other invisible electromagnetic wave obsessed with the building of larger and more requiring massive quantities of gold and silver shrines of the ancient gods, which ruined the national economy and created enemies throughout Egypt. The disks were dismantled during the reign of Tutankhamen, to fund the restoration of the ruined temples of the Ancient gods.

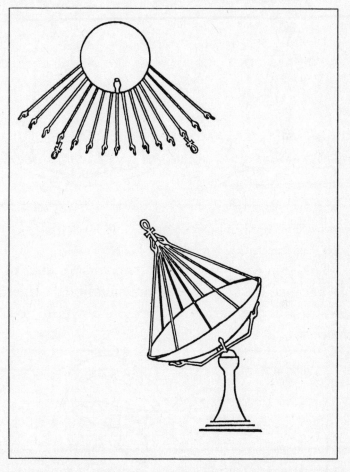

This may be difficult to accept if you are unfamiliar with the two dimensional convention of Egyptian Art as opposed to the modern three dimensional representation.

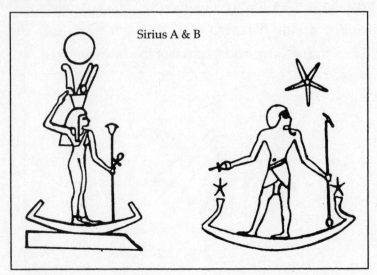

Sirius A & B

Invisible Sirius B was "discovered" in 1970. She is composed of super-dense matter created by an encounter with a black hole.

The Aten was rejected as the universal source of all life because the faintness of the emissions suggested weakness in comparison to the more powerful gods of the past.

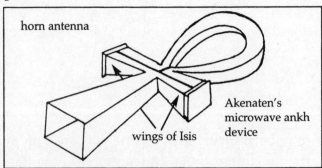

horn antenna

Akenaten's microwave ankh device

wings of Isis

Akenaten's microwave ankh device

The disc of Aten, concentrated the microwave radiation into the horn antenna, exciting the wings of Isis (resonant cavity) into oscillation. The natural frequency of her wings and the incoming microwaves are mixed (heterodyned) and the lower difference frequency, which resulted from the mixing, is detected by the loop. An explanation of the loop's function in this FM discriminator requires an excessive use of technical jargon, which would only detract from the spiritual essence of this divinely inspired device.

This radio telescope could detect radiation from stars and other stellar activities in the cosmos. Akenaten was dismissed as a heretic and is not a favorite among European Egyptologists because of his distinctly African appearance. but he was undoubtedly one of the greatest astronomer- scientists in human history. For he not only discovered the remnants of the Original Spark (the Aten, the Big bang) from which all life originated, but he founded the first religion based on the Oneness of God.

Higher on the electromagnetic frequency scale above microwaves are the invisible infrared rays also known as heat. And by exploring infrared we come to the real reason the pyramids were built.

The word "pyramid" means, fire within (pyr; fire, heat & mid; middle), not the familiar flames, but the Ankhet ☥ living fire." A special fire whose flames were life giving. These rays were concentrated or focused by the pyramid into the sacred chamber under its base.

The pyramid was simply a lens which focused a specific frequency of infrared waves on the sacred chamber.

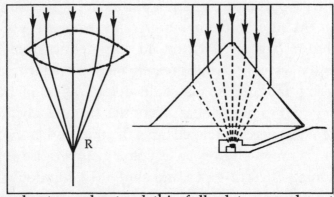

In order to understand this fully, let us explore the question of "living fire."

A by product of both life and combustion is carbon dioxide. If living fire is to exist, carbon dioxide must be eliminated or exhaled and fresh oxygen supplied for further combustion of fuel (organic, fossil or sugar). A flame in an enclosed area would die from the lack of oxygen, which would have been consumed and converted into carbon dioxide.

If carbon dioxide could somehow be converted to it's constituents, carbon and oxygen, the oxygen could be re-used to further continue combustion and produce a living fire.

Carbon dioxide molecules can be split into carbon and oxygen by absorbing energy at specific resonant frequencies. The molecule vibrates in response to the energy absorbed and if there is sufficient concentration of these photons, the molecule splits and oxygen is liberated.

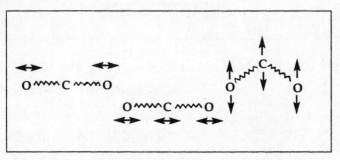

modes of vibration of CO_2

Every object with a temperature above zero degrees Kelvin (K), emits infrared by what is known as Black Body Radiation. The frequency and intensity of the radiation is related to the temperature of the object. At the pyramid's natural temperature of 300 K, there is sufficient infrared at the proper frequency, which the shape of the pyramid can concentrate on the sacred chamber to effect dissociation of carbon dioxide. If the incorrect frequency is used the molecule could split into poisonous carbon monoxide.

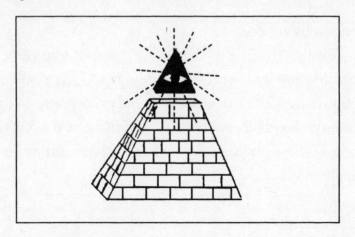

The Sacred Chamber was a special life promoting environment where the dead were revived and incredible surgical procedures could be carried out safely. This technology is specific to Africans, simply because white skin is too reflective and would not allow enough energy to be absorbed.

Imhotep, builder of the first pyramid

The first pyramid was built by Imhotep, the African multi-genius, whom the Greeks called Asclepius, their god of medicine.

114

ASCLEPIUS

Legend has it that Asclepius, god of healing and son of Apollo, was delivered by cesarean section performed on his dead mother Coronis by Thoth (Hermes) and taught the art of medicine. Another version states that he was abandoned on a mountain and suckled by goats. The shepherd who discovered him was frightened when he observed a mysterious aura of glistening corona discharges emanating from the child's skin.

His wisdom and skill in the healing arts were

Thoth

unsurpassed, for Asclepius discovered the secret of the Gorgon's blood, which was both a medicine and a deadly poison. With this knowledge he developed a method of bringing the dead back to life. After reviving many people he himself was killed with a lightning bolt from Zeus, for fear that he might reveal the secret which would give immortality to human beings. Apollo, angered by the

115

murder, responded by killing the thunder-making Cyclopes of Zeus.

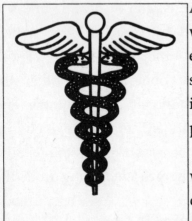

Asclepius was associated with serpents and his emblem of twin winged snakes is still used as the insignia of the medical profession.

Focused infrared rays were also used to dehydrate the bodies of the dead. This sophisticated form of mummification, usually reserved for nobility, produced the most life-like mummies because of the precision of the dehydration process.

However the ultimate use of infrared rays, involved the semiconductor nature of melanin, which requires an infusion of energy to bridge the gap between it's levels of conduction. With this constant source of power the Kha of the Pharaoh would remain an electrically active antenna, supporting his heavenly reflection in divine splendor.

The Ankh of Science

WHEN SANKH WAS HIGH PRIEST, Ankh Science had long ago reached it's zenith in Kemit. The Priesthood of the ☐⚀♀ Ankh, an established University of Ankh Science, maintained the temples and shrines of numerous ankh possessing gods. The most notable of these were the shrine of khonsu, miraculous healing, and Ptah, the god of creative insight. However the Priests of Amen possessed the most powerful shrine, that of spiritual flight or tele-portation. There power arouse from a knowledge of themselves, the knowledge that the photonic essence of man which emanated from the soul was indeed his truest self.

> In him was life, and the life was the light of men. And the light shineth in darkness; and the darkness com-prehended it not.
>
> *St. John 1:4-5*

> The light of the body is the eye: if therefore thine eye be single' thy whole body shall be full of light.
>
> *Matthew 6:22*

After receiving this revelation, I beseeched my lord and master, the High Priest Sankhamen, continually to grant me the knowledge of the secret workings of the ankh of light, which was referred to as the Neb ankh. Understanding of the Neb ankh was achieved at the culmination of a lifetime of study and religious discipline. Although I am only a messenger, with a message already too complex for those who would receive it, I felt compelled to include some mention of it's enormous importance.

The Neb ankh was an awesome experience which would change forever, the initiate's perception of reality. For it was a foretaste of life after death, a discovery of an existence outside the mass of the body, a feeling of total weightlessness and an inter-dimensional access to the Tuat (the otherworld).

Superior African Technology has already achieved levels which are still thought to be science fiction.

The rewards of African Nationalism will be the ability to mount large scale research efforts, akin to the Space Program or the Manhattan Project, to revive ancestral wisdom. Imagine the cohesive power and national unity in Kemit during the Era of Pyramid Building. Modern technology is still in its infancy and can only scratch the surface of this enormously complicated issue. We should abandon the Pale god and return to the worship (study) of Osiris (the Black God, the electronics of Black skin).

Ptah, portrayed as a mummy, with his hands protruding from the wrappings, holding a staff that combines the djed pillar, ankh sign and sceptre.

Although the active component is the melanin granule, its random orientation renders it ineffective. The electromagnetic emissions from the ankh and the uas (scepter) were used to align these tiny dielectric resonator antennas, in order to produce a coherent radiation pattern. The position of a granule can be adjusted. Because, as shown on page 56, the field of a melanin granule could exert a dipole moment on its neighbor, creating the proper alignment of this microscopic antenna array.

119

Coherence is the essential property of a laser (Light Amplification by Stimulated Emission of Radiation), and Black skin can be made to lase.

Light rays, in the form of beams tipped by tiny flames, emitted from the body of Osiris, the Neb Ankh.

Conclusion

THE BASIC CHARACTER OF African Science is the promotion of life, as opposed to the Euro-centric preoccupation with destructive or weapons based technology. Because of this mind-set, the view that all science has some weapons potential, Europeans are intent on suppressing Ankh Science as a matter of National Security. Their need to mis-educate African children results from a very real fear, that the genetic memory of these mental giants will be awakened. This policy has been in effect since the Greeks first encountered this advanced extraterrestrial civilization of the Nile Valley.

Because of the barbaric nature of the Greeks, the Amen Priests were killed, libraries burned, religion distorted and hieroglyphic writing forbidden. This arms race mentality is a permanent feature of Euroscience, having the effect of placing all science under the scrutiny and directorship of the governing body, in order to prevent a departure from science that is only beneficial to Whites. The encounter with an alien civilization, possessing science developed over thousands of years around unique genetic differences, forced Whites to institute policies of mis-education.

The photo-active nature of melanin is an evolutionary quantum-leap, generating a science, culture and religion totally alien to the invaders of the Nile Valley. If allowed unimpeded development, this advantage could be exploited with miraculous consequences for the African, the greatest benefits being in the medical arena, where laser technology and the protein-producing melanocytes will be wedded to create cures unheard of since the time of Imhotep And speaking of Imhotep, could reviving the dead by using infrared laser techniques to dissociate carbon dioxide in the body be far away? This might not be our greatest achievement, for within the genetic memory of an African child is the knowledge to deoxidize melanin and put flesh on dry bones.

Afterword

WHEN I FIRST READ *The Ankh:African origin of Electromagnetism*, I was elated, because all positive information about the Ankh is necessary to awaken the Nubian Kamitik Giants sleeping in the belly of Amenta (the West). The Ankh is the old rugged sign that has been despised by the world. The four major world religions: Hebrew-Israelite, Buddhism, Christianity and Islam were all nurtured by the Ankh people of the Nubian Hapi (Nile) Valley. In this scintillating book, the electromagnetic power of the Ankh has been scientifically investigated by Nur Ankh Amen.

The Egyptological would-be suppressors of AfrakaNubian Spiritual High Kulture continue to deny the primacy of Afrakan Kosmik thought and its application in the mundane realms. These humble Black farmers of the Nile Valley could not possibly have knowledge of electricity and atomic energy. Long before the atom was discovered and misused by western man, Atum appeared on the temple walls of Khamit (Egypt) as the primordial principle of unmanifested potential. It was Atum, cradled on the head of Ptah, the unmoved mover who copulated within her-himself to bring forth Shu-Nifu, the fire fed wind and Tefnut-the materialization of H_2O. These complementary elements sustain the Ankh (Life) principle of the wombniverse.

Nur Ankh Amen has not been criticized because of fear that the reclamation of Ankh Spiritual Science by Afrakan people, will make the foreign imposed religions obsolete. The oppressor knows this much, that the Ankh sign itself is a primordial mental key to unlock the gates of ancestral memory. In his book, *Black Seminarians Without a Black Theology*, Dr. Yosef Ben Jochannan issued a call for restoration of the Ankh to its place of primacy in Afrakan Spiritual High Kulture.

The Ankh is also carried by Nubian Kamitik initiates in the major cities of the West. Bearers of the Ankh are very courageous people who are undaunted by the slander against the Ankh. They have seen beyond the lie that the original AfrakaNubian bearers of the Ankh were 'pagan' and 'heathen' people who 'worshiped idols.' Yet this slander has caused many people of Afrakan ascent to turn away from Ankh science. Bearers of the Ankh are keepers of a sacred legacy which calls them to service as healers in the earth. On the temple walls of Aton-Ra Akhet (called El-Armana today) the Aton Ra (Sun) is chiseled in stone projecting rays terminating in Ankh (Life). The rays of Aton-

Ra are the food of plants. To consume green plants is the way we feed our internal sun within the pineal gland.

The first Ankh bearer was called Heru (in Greek Horus). The aim of all initiates in Ankh Sacred Science is to become transformed into Heru. Heru is the Ankh (Life) advocate ruling the upper realms of your Konsciousness. Heru Asr, the Nubian Falcon of the Holy Spirit, is pictured on temple walls flying with Ankhs in its talons. Heru - the Ankh (Life) messenger came with words of healing and life.

The Socio-Spiritual Meaning of the Ankh

In woman the loop of the Ankh represents the womb, the crossbar the fallopian tubes, the staff the birth canal. In man the loop is his prostate, the crossbar his testes, the staff his penis. Ankh is a life wand. Khamitically speaking our ecological Ankh is that loop of mist drawn up through the power of Aton-Ra's (the Sun's) rays to make clouds which is purified by the Kosmik kiss of Tefnut (moisture). It falls back to earth (the crossbar) as Nun (Rain) or Hapi (die inundated river) fertilizing and bringing the seed of new life (the staff) out of the ground as vegetal food of life in the first times. Ptah's face was green with the promise of renewal and regeneration of life through eating and drinking the green. Queen Afua who as Mut Nebt-Het is Chief Priestess of Purification says,

"Eat green, wear green, walk on green" and Priestess Tehuti adds, "Put green in your pocket." Remember electromagnetic Ankhs utilized copper which is oxidized as green. This is the great drama of the rebirth of Asar the Resurrected One. Ankh is the perennial symbol of the Divine Afrakan family in perpetuity. However you look at it, Ankh is life.

Special Note: For Bearers. Wearers and Keepers of Ankh

Ankhians are not selfish, we share the gifts of healing and life with all people who respect the primordial Aftakan source of all earth life. The mitochondrial Eve is a Nubian Khamit woman - Ta-Urt Sekemet Mut Ast.

The Ankh is an Afrakan re-birth concept and symbol which Afraka gave to the world when she preserved the Ankh on temple walls and as amulets. Ankh may be worn by all who adore NTR the one life source as NTR Ankh (Divine Supreme Womb/Seed Source of Life) the Mother/Father Creator. A wearer of the Ankh is not racist, is not violent, does not eat dead or live animals, nor flesh, avoids any foods that cause putrefaction or fermentation stinking up the body and does not eat creatures with eyes. An initiate wearer, carrier or user of the Ankh honors the feminine (womb) principle as the first and eldest manifestation of divine in Kosmos and on earth. She/he is cognizant of the need of Maat in a patriarchal world. Ankh supporters practice Maatiarchy - balanced

Execution of power in female/male relationships. Ankh demands focus and attention to spiritual and material needs simultaneously.

However you see the Ankh either as a Spiritual, Kultural, healing or scientific tool or wand, it is essential to remember that the Creators of the Ankh instrument caused the rise of the longest lasting most righteous civilization in the Hapi (Nile) Khamitic Valley and sent messengers of Ankh (Life) to all people of earth. So tenacious is humanity's hold on Ankh (Life) that Ankh subliminally creeps up in all English words of continuity. All gerund (ing) words/sounds conceal the Hesi (mantra) Ankh - "ing" is continuity throughout all time and all space. The anchor which secures the lives of passengers on a stormy sea conceals the hesi (word/sound) Ankh. When we thank the Creator, we use the word Ankh. Connect conceals Ankh in the letters "onnec." Our interconnectedness with NTR (Divine) is the greatest lesson taught by Ankh (Life Eternal) science. Ask your k-nee (reverse the sound and the movement). Ask your ankle, ask your tongue which stimulates the waters which form the sound of your voice. Ankh the very word in MTU NTR begins with the wave, (Nu) water. According to Gerrald Massey in Ancient Egypt Light of the World, the very word King conceals the Khamite hope of life eternal. Nkh, Ankh - -g may he live. -g Live the -g.

The Ankh unifies us all in spite of religious and philosophical differences because it is the sign of the Wombniversal AfraKosmik Spiritual source of all religions. Without Ankh (life) of what use is religion? Meditate on ankh as you hesi (chant) Ankh over and over. Come to Ankh. Come to Life.

May this book serve to fill in open gaps in your knowledge. Add this scientific and spiritual portion to your store of Ankh knowledge (reverse the first three letters in know what do you get? Onk, life.) Ink makes the word permanent. The written words of wisdom gives life. I offer this humble addendum as I have been asked. May you take your Ankh back. RISE AFRAKANUBIANKHAMITIKUSHITE PEOPLE, RISE!

Forever yours in Ankhtuity,
For Ankhternity,
Ankhtually,
Heru Ankh Semahj sa Ptah
Studio of Ptah
155 Canal Street, suite 9
New York, NY, 10013
1-212-226-8487
1-212-343-9706

Glossary

ankh: A tau cross with a loop on top.

diety: A person or thing revered to as supremely powerful or beneficent.

djed: Cruciform symbol with at least three cross bars.

lodestone: naturally occurring mineral that is strongly magnetic.

aurora: Intermittent electrical discharge that occurs in the rarefied upper atmosphere.

ionosphere: An ionized layer in a planetary atmosphere where free electrons and ions with thermal energies exist under the control of earth's gravitational and magnetic fields.

ions: electrically charged atoms or group of atoms.

electron: negatively charged elementary particle of the atom.

DNA: The nucleic acid forming the genetic material of all cells.

Heh: God of infinity.

chakras: The points located along the body that are known as energy centers. They are seven of them.

diode An electrical device that allows electricity to flow in one direction only.

SETI: Search for Extraterrestrial Intelligence

UFO Unidentified Flying Object.

Khnum: A Ram-headed creator god often depicted at a potter's wheel fashioning man out of clay.

Hathor: Goddess of jou, love, fertility music and dance and daughter of Ra.

Alchemy: A form of chemistry during the Middle Ages that attempted to discover a method of transmuting base metal into gold.

scepter: A rod or wand held in the hand as a emblem of regal or imperial power.

shrine: Any structure or place that is consecrated or devoted to a holy person or deity.

Egyptology: The science or study of Egyptian antiquities.

capacitor: An arrangement of conductors separated by an insulator (dielectric) used to store charge.

Ptah: Creator God who was usually portrayed as a mummy, with his hands protruding from the wrappings, holding a staff that combines the djed pillar.

Maat: A goddess who personifies the laws of ordered existence.

Tutankhamen: Ruler of the late 18th Dynasty.

Anubis: A god of the dead in the form of a dog or jackal, closely associated with embalming and mummification.

superconductivity: The absence of electrical resistance in certain substances at temperatures close to 0 K.

References

1. Ben-Jochannan, Yosef, Modupe Oduyoye & Charles Finch. *African origins of the Major World Religions.*, Edited by Amon Saba Saakama, 1988.

2. Budge, E. A. Wallis. *Hieroglyphic Dictionary, Vol. 1 & 2.*

————— . *The Mummy A history of the Extraordinary Practices of Ancient Egypt.*

3. *The Holy Bible*, Revised Standard Version. 1952

4. Popular Electronics, July 1990 Oliver Lodge: *Radio's Forgotten Pioneer* by James P Rybak p. 62.

5. Bordeau, Sanford P. *Volts to Hertz the rise of electricity.* 1982.

6. Seffe, Emilio. *From Fallen Bodies to Radio Waves.* University of California, Berkeley.

7. Dakin, H.S. *High Voltage Photography* by , Berkeley, California 1978.

8. Massey, Gerald: *Ancient Egypt Light of the World, Vol. I & 2 & Natural Genesis Vol. 2.*

9. 10. *Treasures of Tutankhamen* Metropolitan Museum of Art. 1976

11. American Scientific, Volume 70. *The Biosynthesis of Mammalian Melanin.* by John M. Pawelek & Ann M. Korner. March-April pg. 136

12. BioScience Vol. 36 No. *What Can We learn From Chick Embryo Melanocytes.* June 1986.

13. *Organic Semiconductors* by Felix Gutmann& Lawrence E. Lyons.

14. Blake, George G. *History of Radio Telegraphy and Telegraphy*. by

15. Phillips, Vivian J., *Early Radio Waves Detectors*. Institution of Electrical Engineering, London & N.Y. 1980.

16. *Syntony and Spark. the origins of Radio*. Hugh G. J. Aitken. Princeton University Press. 1975.

17. Gottlieb, Irving M, *Understanding Oscillators* by

18. Chambers, R. G. *Molecular Semiconductors* (Physics and its applications 1.)

20. *Neural Network Architecture*, an introduction by Judith E. Dayhoff.

21. Cheikh Anta Diop, *Great African Thinkers* edited Ivan Van Sertima.

22. Cress Welsing, Dr. Frances, *The Isis Papers*.

Index

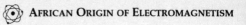

THE ANKH ☥

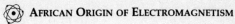

EWorld Inc.
Send for our complete full color catalog today!

A BOOK OF THE BEGINNINGS VOL. I & II (SET).................*MASSEY*.........................49.95
AFRIKAN HOLISTIC HEALTH ....*AFRIKA*........................19.95
AFRICAN DISCOVERY OF AMERICA.................................*WEINER*........................15.95
ANACALYPSIS (SET)...*MASSEY*.........................49.95
ARAB INVASION OF EGYPT 16.95
ANKH: AFRICAN ORIGIN OF ELECTROMAGNETISM 10.95
AIDS THE END OF CIVILIZATION...*DOUGLASS*....................9.95
BABY NAMES:REAL NAMES WITH REAL MEANINGS FOR AFRICAN CHILDREN...........12.95
BLACK HEROES OF THE MARTIAL ARTS ....*VAN CLIEF*...................16.95
APOCRYPHA (HC) 14.95
BRITISH HISTORIANS & THE WEST INDIES ....*ERIC WILLIAMS*.........14.95
CHRISTOPHER COLUMBUS & THE AFRICAN HOLOCAUST   *JOHN HENRIK CLARKE*.....10.95
COLUMBUS CONSPIRACY...*BRADLEY*...................14.95
DAWN VOYAGE:THE BLACK AFRICAN DISCOVERY OF AMERICA............*BRADLEY*.....14.95
DOCUMENTS OF WEST INDIAN HISTORY ....*ERIC WILLIAMS*.........15.95
EDUCATION OF THE NEGRO.................................*CARTER G. WOODSON*..............14.95
EGYPTIAN BOOK OF THE DEAD...*BUDGE*......................16.95
EGYPTIAN BOOK OF THE DEAD/ANCIENT MYSTERIES OF AMENTA *MASSEY*.............9.95
FIRST COUNCIL OF NICE: A WORLD'S CHRISTIAN CONVENTION A.D. 325 ....10.95
FORBIDDEN BOOKS OF THE NEW TESTAMENT..14.95
GERALD MASSEY'S LECTURES 10.95
GLOBAL AFRIKAN PRESENCE..................................*EDWARD SCOBIE*...................15.95
GOSPEL OF BARNABAS 14.95
GREATER KEY OF SOLOMON 10.00
HAIRLOCKING: EVERYTHING YOU NEED TO KNOW ....*NEKHENA EVANS*...................9.95
HARLEM VOICES FROM THE SOUL OF BLACK AMERICA *JOHN HENRIK CLARKE*........10.95
HARLEM USA ....*JOHN HENRIK CLARKE*..........10.95
HEAL THYSELF FOR HEALTH AND LONGEVITY ....*QUEEN AFUA* 18.95
HEAL THYSELF COOKBOOK:HOLISTIC COOKING WITH JUICES ....*DIANE CICCONE* 13.95
HISTORICAL JESUS & THE MYTHICAL CHRIST ....*GERALD MASSEY*.........9.95
HISTORY OF THE PEOPLE OF TRINIDAD & TOBAGO ....*ERIC WILLIAMS* 15.95
LOST BOOKS OF THE BIBLE & THE FORGOTTEN BOOKS OF EDEN 14.95
NUTRITION MADE SIMPLE; AT A GLANCE 8.95
SIGNS & SYMBOLS OF PRIMORDIAL MAN 17.95
VITAMINS & MINERALS A TO Z ....*JEWEL POOKRUM*.............13.95
WHAT THEY NEVER TOLD YOU IN HISTORY CLASS VOL. ONE ....*CUSH*...............19.95
FREEMASONRY INTERPRETED 12.95
FREEMASONRY & THE VATICAN 11.95
FREEMASONRY & JUDAISM 11.95
FREEMASONRY:CHARACTER CLAIMS...13.95
FREEMASONRY EXPOSITION: EXPOSITION & ILLUSTRATIONS OF FREEMASONRY.............9.95
SCIENCE OF MELANIN...14.95
SECRET SOCIETIES & SUBVERSIVE MOVEMENTS...13.95

Prices subject to change without notice

Mail To: EWorld Inc. – 1200 Jefferson Ave. – Buffalo – New York – 14208
TEL:(716) 882-1704 FAX: (716) 882-1708 EMAIL: eeworldinc@yahoo.com
NAME:_____
ADDRESS_____
CITY_____ST_____ZIP_____